T0315266

Managing Stakeholders in Software Development Projects

Dedicated to my late Father sadly missed by all his family

Managing Stakeholders in Software Development Projects

John McManus

 Routledge
Taylor & Francis Group

LONDON AND NEW YORK

First published 2005 by Butterworth-Heinemann

2 Park Square, Milton Park, Abingdon, Oxon OX14 4RN
711 Third Avenue, New York, NY 10017, USA

Routledge is an imprint of the Taylor & Francis Group, an informa business

First issued in hardback 2017

British Library Cataloguing in Publication Data
A catalogue record for this book is available from the British Library

ISBN 978-0-7506-6455-4 (pbk)
ISBN 978-1-138-43537-7 (hbk)

Composition by Charon Tec Pvt. Ltd, Chennai, India

Contents

Contents

Computer Weekly Professional Series

There are few professions which require as much continuous updating as that of the IS executive. Not only does the hardware and software scene change relentlessly, but also ideas about the actual management of the IS function are being continuously modified, updated and changed. Thus keeping abreast of what is going on is really a major task.

Computer Weekly Professional Series has been created to assist IS executives keep up-to-date with the management ideas and issues of which they need to be aware.

One of the key objectives of the series is to reduce the time it takes for leading edge management ideas to move from the academic and consulting environments into the hands of the IT practitioner. Thus this series employs appropriate technology to speed up the publishing process. Where appropriate some books are supported by CD-ROM or by additional information or templates located on the Web.

This series provides IT professionals with an opportunity to build up a bookcase of easily accessible, but detailed information on the important issues that they need to be aware of to successfully perform their jobs.

Aspiring or already established authors are invited to get in touch with me directly if they would like to be published in this series.

Dr Dan Remenyi
Series Editor
dan.remenyi@mcil.co.uk

ix

Other titles in the Series

x

Preface

As stakeholder relationships and business in general have become increasingly central to the unfolding of stakeholder thinking, important new topics have begun to take centre stage in both the worlds of practitioners and academics. For example, within the global software industry the evolution of stakeholder thinking has led to a new view of the project organization embedded in a complex web of relationships and interrelationships. This concept of the project organization is consistent with recent advances in organization theory and highlights the symbiotic nature of relationship between project and stakeholder. Consequently, this view moves beyond stakeholder management to emphasis new concerns such as project management engagement with stakeholders and stakeholder responsibilities.

The role of project management becomes immeasurably more challenging, when stakeholders are no longer seen as simple objects of managerial action but rather as subjects with their own objectives and purposes.

A stakeholder is anyone who is involved in, or affected by, a project or programme, and that is potentially a lot of people. As we will see, stakeholders come in all shapes and sizes. Some are actively involved in the project; others are passive bystanders who will be affected by the performance of, or the end product of, the project. We stand the greatest chance of success if all our stakeholders are working in harmony with a common understanding of the project's objectives and commitment to them.

This book will aim to explain some of the complexities of project management and managerial relationships with stakeholders by discussing the practice of stakeholder engagement, dialogue, ethics, measurement and management, and the consequences of this practice for reporting and productivity, and performance within project management.

This text presents emerging concepts in stakeholder management that are largely ignored in other texts on project management. One example is the unified theory of stakeholder management outlined in Chapters 1–3. The other is the discussion on project governance in Chapter 4. The topics discussed are mapped within the *Taxonomy Stakeholder Model – D1, Stakeholder Analysis Model – D2, and the Software Project Model – D3*. The book is divided into seven chapters; all chapters are written from a practitioner perspective (but material is drawn from the world of academia where appropriate). The last chapter is a collection of short essays, which have been included to reinforce specific points and highlight different approaches to stakeholder management in different business sectors.

In writing this book I have attempted to draw on my practical experience and where appropriate those of other practitioners working within the software industry. The summary points at the end of each chapter serve as a review guide or may be used by the reader as a framework for discussion. Whilst I have attempted to refrain from duplication, some duplication within chapters is inevitable. I believe however, that this helps the reader by strengthening the points made in previous chapters. Where appropriate to do so, I have used the terms "software project manager" and "project manager" interchangeably throughout the book. In essence, however, they are the same entity.

John McManus

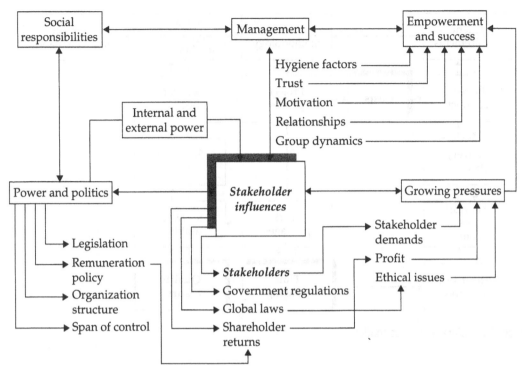

Figure D1 Taxonomy stakeholder model.

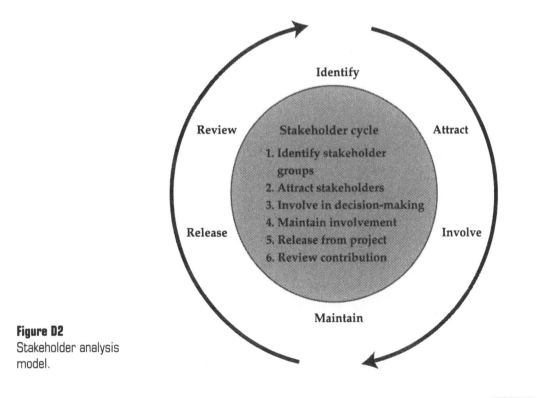

Figure D2
Stakeholder analysis
model.

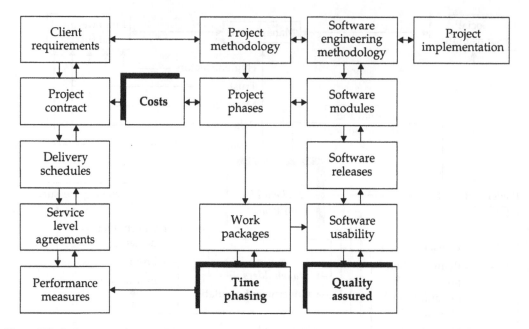

Figure D3 Software project model.

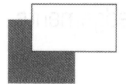

About the author

John McManus is a software engineer with 15 years experience in project delivery and is an acknowledged expert in project recovery methods and risk management. John is Professor in Management Sciences at the Rushmore Institute.

Acknowledgements

In the preparation of this book I would like to acknowledge a few people David R. Beatty, OBE, Director Clarkson Centre, Scott Ambler, Senior Consultant, Ronin International, Inc, Les Stahike, President Governance Matters. COM, Robin Dudash, Innovative Quality Products and Systems, Deborah Vogwell of Davis Langdon Everest, Douglas Wood, NAVIGATE Consulting, Karl Wiegers, Process Impact, Joanna Rothman, Mike Cash and the Production Team at Elsevier Butterworth-Heinemann – I thank all and every one of you for your generosity, help, and assistance in getting this project into print.

John McManus

Princes (and Project Managers)

I pour myself out as fully as I can in meditation on the subject, discussing what a principality is, what kinds there are, how they can be acquired, how they can be kept, why they are lost: and if any of my fancies ever pleased you, this ought not to displease you: and to a prince, especially to a new one, it should be welcome: therefore I dedicate it to his Magnificence Giuliano.

Nicolo Machiavelli Archive, 1439–1527 (Florence).

1   Stakeholders and the Context of Software Project Management

1.1 Software project management

Software project managers are frequently called upon to manage and deliver many different types of projects. While the specifics of these projects may vary, one constant remains that is the manner in which a project is first communicated and addressed to its stakeholders will greatly influence the likelihood of its success.

Any software project has two main activity streams: engineering and project management. The engineering activity is concerned with building the system (or artefact) and focuses on those software issues as how to design, code, and test. The project management activity is largely concerned with risk, cost, and quality. To this end successful project management depends not on the type of technical project, but on consistently applying the right project and people methodologies. Methodologies provide the cornerstone by which we can plan, execute, measure, monitor, control, and reduce project risk. According to the Standish Group: *formal methodology provides a realistic picture of the project and resources committed to it, and it results in steps and procedures the team can reproduce and reuse.* It also enables the team to maximize consistency and it incorporates lessons learned into active projects. Methodologies encourage go or no-go decision checkpoints. They also help the project team proceed with a higher level of confidence, or halt or alter steps to fit changing requirements. Figure 1.1 provides one view of an integrated stakeholder and project management framework.

In the last decade project management theory has to some extent concentrated on the questions of structure, control, and monitoring. For a project manager, the structure of a given project is

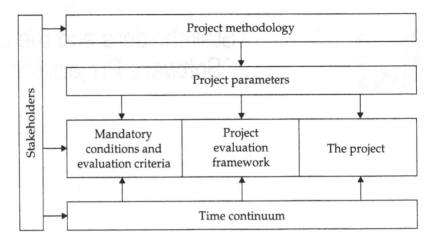

Figure 1.1
A project
stakeholder
framework.

often imposed and often stands at odds with the environment into which this structure is to be transplanted. It is the craft of the project manager to improvise within this imposed structure according to the demands of the environment and the stakeholders who are inherent within it.

What is distinctive for projects is their parameters. Parameters are not static entities, but more of an existential condition of knowing that the defining characteristic for one's actions is their connection to a predetermined goal, be this goal of time, cost, or quality. But, even though a project by definition is usually a planned, scripted activity, it is the definitional characteristic of uniqueness that exerts the most influence over the actual network of activities that becomes the project. One can plan a project forever, but the project execution will still be at the mercy of the uniqueness that, in a way, is the project.

The management of software projects is a less straightforward activity than is usually assumed in the literature. This management is less a following of a project plan, and more the handling of continuous action, some ordered, some not. In the case of complex projects, such as the design and build of an entirely new software system, innovation must be at the forefront of a project managers thinking. A recurring theme in project management is that performance and success are closely related to innovative (or lateral) thinking and project management capability.

One manager and educator Edward de Bono has written extensively about the process of lateral thinking. De Bono identifies four critical factors associated with lateral thinking: (1) recognize dominant ideas that polarize perception of a problem,

(2) searching for different ways of looking at things, (3) relaxation of rigid control of thinking, and (4) use of chance to encourage other ideas. This last factor has to do with the fact that lateral thinking involves low-probability ideas, which are unlikely to occur in the normal course of events. I return to this subject in Section 3.6.1.

(See De Bono, E. (1991) Teaching Thinking. London, Penguin Books.)

Project failure at times is associated with poor decision-making and lack of stakeholder involvement in searching for solutions to project management problems. One thing I learned from reading De Bono's works is that an attitude of continuing to search for a solution, even when it seems quite impossible, often does lead to a solution, you must include your key stakeholders, and inclusion is a must.

Research undertaken by McManus and Wood-Harper (2003) for their book *Information Systems Project Management* noted that relationship and stakeholder management were the key factors mitigating failure and reducing project risk. Key points noted in relation to stakeholder management and project failure include:

- Failure to manage stakeholder expectations
- Failure to share knowledge with stakeholders
- Failure to share bad news with stakeholders
- Lack of project leadership (too much reinventing the wheel)
- Lack of shared information, that is:
  - What information is needed?
  - What level of urgency?
  - Who needs it?
  - When or how frequently is it to be produced?
  - In what form or way will it be sent?
  - Where is it to be kept?
- Lack of team motivation to undertake work
- Lack of communication and co-ordination, that is lack of management strategy to deliver the project.

In larger companies only 9% of the projects come in on time and on budget. Failed projects exhibit all or many of the above symptoms, but arguably *the most important flaw* in failed projects is the failure to manage stakeholder expectations.

(Source: The Standish Group, as reported by Solutions Integrator, June 30, 1999.)

1.1.1 The right project methodology

With the exclusion of PRINCE2 (which I will come back to in Chapter 2) most of the current thinking about how to deliver software engineering projects has come from *Specialist Interest Groups* (or SIGs) or individual software professionals. The ideas they developed have proven to be quite effective when used by small to medium organizations to create custom methodologies. Even though the best ideas could also be applied to projects undertaken by larger system integrators to date this has not tended to happen. Why? Structure and the imposition of non-valued management would seem to be major obstacles together with poor judgement and lack of control where it really matters at the coalface.

Advances in methodologies such as the Dynamic Systems Development Method (DSDM), Rational Unified Process (RUP), and lightweight approaches such as eXtreme Programming (XP), Crystal and Scrum place significant currency on user participation, and stakeholder involvement. Taken together, the current methodologies offer a wide range of choices to meet the particular needs of many software projects and the skill level of any organization. The most important reason for undertaking software projects is to improve the way a business process is performed. Software projects should follow a disciplined methodology. Common to many of these methods are the following attributes:

- Business vision
- Business models
- Configuration management
- Communication
- Contingency planning
- Data entry standards
- Development models
- Documentation
- Metrics
- Project plans
- Performance criteria
- Quality assurance
- Risk planning
- Software standards
- Software process
- Software testing
- Support tools
- Stakeholders
- Team structures.

(See McManus, J. (2003) System Development, Team Agility. The Computer Bulletin, pp. 26–27.)

For completeness I would like to discuss each of these methods in brief. Starting with DSDM.

1.1.1.1 DSDM overview

The DSDM method is based on nine principles, these principles include:

1. Active user involvement
2. Teams must be empowered to make decisions
3. Focus is on frequent delivery of software products
4. Fitness of business purpose is the key criterion
5. Iterative and incremental development is necessary
6. All changes are reversible
7. Requirements are baseline at a high level
8. Testing is integrated throughout the life cycle
9. Collaborative and co-operative approach between stake-holders is essential.

1.1.1.2 RUP overview

The RUP method addresses the issues on how object-oriented development works. The principles include:

1. The process is iterative and incremental development process
2. The method allows increasing understanding of the problem through successive refinement
3. The method gives an effective solution and multiple iterations
4. The method consists of four phases: inception, elaboration, construction, and transition:
   - *Inception:* establishes the business rational for the project
   - *Elaboration:* collects detailed requirements to establish an architecture baseline and create a plan for construction
   - *Construction:* consists of many iterations, in which each iteration analyses designs, builds, tests, and integrates a subset of requirements of a project
   - *Transition:* includes beta testing, packaging, performance tuning, and training
5. The method relies on iterative user involvement and collective risk assessment methods.

1.1.1.3 XP overview

XP is a lightweight discipline of software development based on principles of simplicity, communication, feedback, and courage. XP is designed for use with small teams who need to develop software quickly in an environment of rapidly changing requirements. The method subscribes to the values of simplicity, communication, feedback, and courage. XP currently recommends 12 practices to support the four values:

1. *Planning*: the XP planning process allows the XP "customer" to define the business value of desired features, and uses cost estimates provided by the programmers, to choose what needs to be done and what needs to be deferred. The effect of XP's planning process is that it is easy to steer the project to success.
2. *Small releases*: XP teams put a simple system into production early, and update it frequently on a very short cycle. Cycles lengths of a couple of months are recommended. This allows the business value of the product to be evaluated in the real world.
3. *Metaphor*: XP teams use a common system of names and a common system description that guide development and communication.
4. *Simple design*: a program should be the simplest one that meets the current requirements. There is not much building "for the future". The focus is on providing business value. Of course, it is necessary to ensure that you have a good design. In XP this is achieved through relentless refactoring.
5. *Testing*: XP teams focus on validation of the software at all times. Programmers develop software by writing tests first, then software that fulfils the requirements reflected in the tests. Customers provide acceptance tests in advance of development that enable them to be certain that the features they need are provided.
6. *Refactoring*: XP teams improve the design of the system throughout the entire development cycle. Keeping the software clean does this: without duplication, with high communication, simple, yet complete. All code should be refactored as often as possible. Refactoring is a process of improving a program's structure without changing its functionality.
7. *Pair programming*: XP programmers write all production code in pairs, two programmers working together at one machine. Pair members rotate regularly. Less experienced members are constantly mentored, and the risk of less experienced code being added to the application is minimized.

Pair programming provides constant code reviews. No more dreary code review meetings – put two sets of eyes on the code as it is written. Experiments have shown that pair programming produces betters software at similar or lower cost than programmers working alone.

8. *Collective ownership*: all the code belongs to all the programmers. This means anyone is authorized to improve any part of it at any time. This lets the team go at full speed, because when something needs changing, it can be changed without delay. Collective ownership of the code by all members of the team helps ensure even more eyes will see the code, increasing the amount of code review performed.

9. *Continuous integration*: XP teams integrate and build the software system multiple times per day. This keeps all the programmers on the same page, and enables very rapid progress. Integrating frequently tends to eliminate integration problems that plague teams who integrate less often.

10. *Forty-hour week*: tired programmers make more mistakes. XP teams do not work excessive overtime, keeping them fresh, healthy, and effective.

11. *On-site customer*: an XP project is steered by a dedicated individual who is empowered to determine requirements, set priorities, and answer questions as the programmers have them. The effect of being there is that communication improves, with less hard-copy documentation – often one of the most expensive parts of a software project. Ideally, the customer sits at a desk next to the programmers for the length of the project.

12. *Coding standard*: for a team to work effectively in pairs, and to share ownership of all the code, all the programmers need to write the code in the same way, with rules that make sure the code communicates clearly.

1.1.1.4 Crystal overview

Crystal collects together self-adapting family of "shrink-to-fit", human-powered software development methodologies based on these understandings:

1. Every project needs a slightly different set of policies and conventions, or methodology.
2. The workings of the project are sensitive to people issues, and improve as the people issues improve, individuals get better, and their teamwork gets better.
3. Better communications and frequent deliveries communication reduce the need for intermediate work products.

Crystal is a family of human-powered and adaptive, ultra light, "shrink-to-fit" software development methodologies. "Human-powered" means that the focus is on achieving project success through enhancing the work of the people involved (other methodologies might be process-centric, or architecture-centric, or tool-centric, but Crystal is people-centric). "Ultra light" means that for whatever the project size and priorities, a Crystal-family methodology for the project will work to reduce the paperwork, overhead and bureaucracy to the least that is practical for the parameters of that project. "Shrink-to-fit" means that you start with something small enough, and work to make it smaller and better fitting. Crystal is non-jealous, meaning that a Crystal methodology permits substitution of similar elements from other methodologies. Key points are:

- two base techniques: methodology tuning technique, and reflection workshop technique retrospective
- incremental development of 4 months or less
- clear ownership model of work products
- have regression testing.

Crystal is evolving in tandem with the understanding of the principles of lightweight software development processes and people-centric project management. It aligns itself with the manifesto for software development (refer to *Agile Software Development* by Alistair Cockburn, 2001).

1.1.1.5 Scrum overview

Scrum as applied to software development was first referred to in "The New Product Development Game" (*Harvard Business Review*, 86116, 137–146, 1986) and later elaborated in "The Knowledge Creating Company" both by Ikujiro Nonaka and Hirotaka Takeuchi (Oxford University Press, 1995).

Scrum is an iterative, incremental process for developing any product or managing any work. It produces a set of functionality at the end of every iteration. Its key attributes are as follows. Scrum is:

- an agile process to manage and control development work
- a wrapper for existing engineering practices
- a team-based approach to iteratively, incrementally develop systems and products when requirements are rapidly changing

- a process that controls the chaos of conflicting interests and needs
- a way to improve communications and maximize co-operation
- a way to detect and cause the removal of anything that gets in the way of developing and delivering products
- a way to maximize productivity
- scalable from single projects to entire organizations and has controlled and organized development and implementation for multiple interrelated products and projects with over a thousand developers and implementers
- a way for everyone to feel good about their job, their contributions, and that they have done the very best they possibly could.

Scrum's goal is to deliver as much quality software as possible within a series (3–8), of short time-boxes (fixed time intervals) called *Sprints* that typically last about a month. Each stage in the development cycle (requirements, analysis, design, evolution, and delivery) is now mapped to a *Sprint* or series of *Sprints*. The traditional software development stages are retained for convenience primarily for tracking milestones. So, for example, the requirements stage may use one *Sprint*, including the delivery of a prototype. The analysis and design stages may take one *Sprint* each. While the evolution stage may take anywhere from three to five *Sprints*.

As opposed to a repeatable and defined process approach, in Scrum there is no predefined process within a *Sprint*. Instead, *Scrum Meetings* drive the completion of the allocated activities. Each *Sprint* operates on a number of work items called a *Backlog*. As a rule, no more items are externally added into the *Backlog* within a *Sprint*. Internal items resulting from the original pre-allocated *Backlog* can be added to it. The goal of a *Sprint* is to complete as much quality software as possible.

The Scrum process is fully described in the book *Agile Software Development with Scrum* by Ken Schwaber and Mike Beedle (Prentice Hall, 2001), from which this paragraph was summarized.

1.1.2 The right project team

In software engineering projects considerable effort is expended in the analysis and design phases. These phases require creative and talented people, I have always adhered to the maxim that talented people can make just about anything happen (provided they have stakeholder support) and although this is not always popular with managers who allocate resources I believe it holds up when delivering complex projects.

Identifying people with the right technical and soft skills for the project is a key challenge for many project managers. Selecting people to fill key roles in projects is not always easy especially when multiple projects are on the go or when the organization is contracting. Key positions to fill will most certainly include:

- Deputy project manager
- Quality assurance manager
- Technical design authority
- Technical designers
- Software developers
- Business analysts and modelers
- Configuration manager
- Business user
- Domain expert
- Sponsors representatives.

While no single selection process is guaranteed to deliver the people you are looking for, the project manager should try to minimize the risk by having a multiple selection process. Most software projects require people to work together in small groups for intensive periods of time. To do this effectively it is useful to understand something about how individuals may behave towards each other and within the project in different situations. Belbin as devised a questionnaire to ascertain the mix of personality types (and soft skills) that make up a balanced team. Belbin identifies nine roles (Figure 1.2). The Belbin role types include: plant, resource investigator, co-ordinator, shaper, monitor/evaluator, team worker, implementer, completer, and specialist. Generally project teams work best when they have a good balance of the nine roles.

1.1.3 The right project manager

From an organization, client and stakeholder perspective, selecting the right project manager is critical. When senior management selects a project manager several factors should be considered. For example, project managers working within the software industry must possess a high level of technical competence. Required skills and knowledge include: an understanding of software risk, and of the technology of software engineering,

Role	Description of role traits
Plant	*Positives* Creative, imaginative, and unorthodox. Can solve difficult problems. *Negatives* Ignores details and can be too pre-occupied to communicate effectively.
Resource investigator	*Positives* An extrovert, enthusiastic, and communicative. Develops contacts. *Negatives* Can be overly optimistic, and may lose interest once initial enthusiasm has passed.
Co-ordinator	*Positives* Mature, confidant, and a good chairperson. Clarifies goals, promotes decision-making and delegates well. *Negatives* Can be seen as manipulative; delegates personal work.
Shaper	*Positives* Challenging, dynamic, and thrives on pressure. Has the drive and courage to overcome obstacles. *Negatives* Can provoke others and hurt their feelings.
Monitor/evaluator	*Positives* Sober, strategic, and discerning, sees all options and judges accurately. *Negatives* May lack drive and ability to inspire others and be overly critical.
Team worker	*Positives* Co-operative, mild, perceptive, and diplomatic. Listens, builds, averts friction, calms the waters. *Negatives* May be indecisive in crunch times, and can be easily influenced.
Implementer	*Positives* Disciplined, reliable, conservative, and efficient. Turns ideas into practical actions. *Negatives* Somewhat inflexible; slow to respond to new possibilities.
Completer	*Positives* Painstaking, conscientious, and anxious; searches out errors and omissions. Delivers on time. *Negatives* Inclined to worry too much. Reluctant to delegate. Can be a nitpicker.
Specialist	*Positives* Single-minded, self-starting, and dedicated. Provides knowledge and skills in rare supply. *Negatives* Contributes on only a narrow front. Dwells on technicalities. Overlooks the "big picture".

Figure 1.2 Belbin roles.

(Figure 1.2 is adapted from Belbin, R.M. (1993) Team Roles at Work, Butterworth Heinemann, 1993.)

awareness of programming tools and techniques used in software development, knowledge of current analysis methods, and knowledge of project management techniques. Project managers need not necessarily be technical experts in all aspects of a project. Of course, the project manager should also have above average diplomacy and managerial abilities.

While all this seems obvious, according to research many project managers are perceived to be average or below average in the areas of leadership skills, interpersonal relationships, and administration.

Because there is a high correlation between the quality level of the attributes needed of project managers and the use of soft skills, careful analysis of the project managers' managerial experience and capability of working with different stakeholder groups should be confirmed prior to selection or appointment.

One characteristic a project manager must possess is the ability to see the "big picture". Successful project managers recognize that many factors affect the outcome of a project. They must consider not only the technical aspects but also the economic, social, and legal aspects. Their perspective must be broad, seeing the whole picture, and requires taking a holistic approach. It is argued by *McManus and Wood-Harper* that many project managers lack this characteristic. They often fall into the trap of emphasizing the technical side while neglecting other important areas. As a result, relations with stakeholders often deteriorate. This may lead to legal complications rising due to lack of compliance and trust.

(Source: McManus, J., and T. Wood-Harper (2003) Information Systems Project Management, FT Prentice Hall, p. 39.)

1.2 The nature of stakeholder theory

The best way to begin to develop a stakeholder approach line of thinking is to start at the beginning with some theory. Edward Freeman, a major protagonist in the stakeholder literature has developed a stakeholder theory of a modern corporation which includes owners, suppliers, employees, customers, local communities, and managers that are considered to be the primary stakeholders to which an organization as a moral responsibility (Freeman, 1984; 1997). A wider definition of stakeholders would include any group or individual who can affect or is affected by the achievement of the organization's objectives (Freeman, 1984, p. 46). In organizations that use traditional project management methodologies such as PRINCE2, stakeholders are normally defined as internal (direct) and external (indirect). Those directly affected by a proposed project are clearly among the key stakeholders. They are the ones who stand to benefit or lose from the organizations operations or who warrant redress from any negative effects of such operations. It is these directly affected stakeholders, who are the most significant and occasionally the most difficult to identify and involve in participatory efforts.

(The term PRINCE2 stands for Projects in a Controlled Environment and is the UK's defacto project management methodology.)

1.2.1 Identifying stakeholders

In many software project stakeholders are numerous and sometimes difficult to identify. One method for identifying stakeholders is the use of a "contrast" or "maximum" variation sampling procedure. This can be used to define local groupings around project issues. Each potential stakeholder is interviewed and asked to identify another who will have the most different perceptions on the issue than his/her own. The process of interviewing and identifying new respondents with contrasting views is repeated until several main issues or themes emerge. These themes each represent a stakeholder group. This approach enables the identification of stakeholder groups with conflicting or different values without asking direct questions that may be socially unacceptable to answer. See also Section 2.1.1.

Another approach to stakeholder identification is to produce a stakeholder map. Figure 1.3 identifies key stakeholder groups and organizations that will be included in an National Health

Figure 1.3
Simple example of key stakeholder map. (GPs, general practitioners; PCTs, patient-controlled trials.)

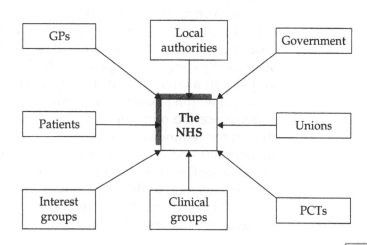

13

Service (NHS) project. All of these parties have a stake in the successful implementation of a project, so it is important to identify which stakeholders will have an impact on the work of the project team. For example, at the final implementation phase of a project, the potential for misuse and malfunction of a proposed software system must be analysed in terms of its impact on all of the projects present and future stakeholders.

As pointed out in Section 1.1.2, a typical software project team consists of a project manager, analysts, designers, developers, testers, and quality assurance personnel. The team may also include users or their representatives. Unfortunately, the literature on software project management often fails to clearly classify types of stakeholders and to describe strategies for their management. For example, Mitchell *et al.* (1997), give a list of 27 definitions of the term stakeholder used from 1993 to 1995 showing the intention of researchers to answer the fundamental question of which entities can be defined as stakeholders that deserve the managers' attention. A stakeholders' significance will depend upon the situation and the issues encountered during the project life cycle. Of all the possible stakeholders (see example in Figure 1.4), the ones who will be relevant to the organization's management team will depend on the particular problem. The bigger, the more complex the problem, the more it is likely to involve a wider array of stakeholders. As a result, the more assumptions needed. It is characteristic and fundamental feature of complex problems that not everything of basic importance can be known prior to working on the problem. Rather, such a statement often only emerges with difficulty over time and only as a direct result of our working on it. In such circumstances both the stakeholders' motivation and opportunity to act are particularly sensitive to specific issues (Freeman, 1984). The motivation of stakeholders for their contribution can vary considerably; for example, the customer would like to introduce change with maximum benefit, the project manager wants to successfully complete the project with the appropriate resources, and the an analyst would like to specify the requirements on time and within budget. Stakeholders have various possibilities to influence the outcome of the project life cycle, for example during the requirements analysis (and evaluation) stage stakeholders can and do manipulate the requirements specification to articulate their own interests. Davis (1982, p. 10), names some cognitive aspects to this bias. Stakeholders tend to rate current information higher than less recent information, they base their judgement on information available, are particularly influenced

Software project life cycle stage	Primary, secondary, external, and extended stakeholders	
1. System requirements analysis 2. System architectural design 3. Software requirements analysis 4. Software architectural design 5. Software detailed design 6. Software coding and testing 7. Software integration 8. Software qualification testing 9. System integration 10. System testing 11. Software installation 12. Acceptance support	• Project board member's • Non-executive directors • Manager/director • Department manager • Account managers • Project sponsor • Champion user • Human resources manager • Department users • Programme manager • Project manager • Business architect • Business analysts • Technical architect • Database architect • Database analyst • Developers • Integration manager • Configuration manager • Change control manager • QA manager • Test manager • Testers • Infrastructure support teams • Software support team	• Government minister • Government agencies • MPs and MEPs • Local authorities • Statutory and voluntary agencies • Private sector agencies • Professional regulatory bodies, e.g. GMC • Financial institutions • Unions, e.g. UNISON • Public relations • Local interest groups • Patients • General public • GP's • Clinical staff • Consultants • Ambulance service • Safety advisors

Figure 1.4 Example of stakeholders involved in NHS-related software projects. (MPs, Members of Parliament; MEP, Members of European Parliament; GMC, General Medical Council; QA, quality assurance.)

by recent events and are not good at as intuitive statisticians so that they draw unwarranted conclusions from small samples or a small number of occurrences. Another major influence results from personal interests within the issues touched by the object or situation to be evaluated. Blumberg and Gerwin (1981) note: *Managers (and other stakeholders) do not have the expertise to second-guess the judgements of technical experts when evaluating whether or not to purchase equipment (IT solutions). Consequently, they tend to employ mainly financial criteria in judging requirements.*

1.2.2 Supportive stakeholder relationships

There are many reasons to believe that adoption of a stake-holder approach to software project management and management in general will contribute to the long-term survival and success of a project organization. Positive and mutually support-ive stakeholder relationships encourage trust, and stimulate

Principle	Condition	Narration
1	Monitor	Managers have moral obligation to monitor the concerns of legitimate stakeholders and to take their interests into account
2	Communicate	Managers should keep an open mind when making decisions and activity involve stakeholders in the decision-making process
3	Behaviour	Managers should support processes and modes of behaviour that are sympathetic, sensitive, and respectful to stakeholders and their needs
4	Risk	Managers should recognize the individual stakeholder sacrifices and take positive steps to ensure that an just risk reward strategy is implemented
5	Co-operation	Managers should work to harmonize events that may destabilize stakeholder involvement
6	Rights	Managers should avoid activities that jeopardize human rights or give rise to risks that are unacceptable to stakeholders
7	Conflict	Managers have moral and legal responsibilities to stakeholders and should address conflicts through open communication

Figure 1.5 Clarkson's principles of stakeholder management.

(Figure 1.5 is adapted from Clarkson, M. (1995) A stakeholder framework for analyzing and evaluating corporate social performance. Academy of Management Review, 20, 92–117.)

collaborative efforts that lead to relational wealth, that is organizational assets arising from familiarity and teamwork. By contrast, conflict and suspicion stimulate formal bargaining and limit efforts and rewards to teams, which result in time delays and increased costs. In addition, more and more managers are recognizing that a reputation for "ethical and socially responsible behaviour" can be the basis for a competitive edge in both market and public policy relationships. Finally, in spite of the specification and measurement difficulties involved, research studies have found evidence of positive associations (few have found negative associations) between various socially and ethically responsible practices and conventional economic and financial indicators of performance (profitability, growth, etc.) Thus, there is no reason to think that the conscientious and continuing practice of stakeholder management will conflict with conventional financial performance goals see Figure 1.5.

In the world of software projects, project managers tend to hold high office and may be regarded as *Captains* of the project organization. Jones (see Hill and Jones, 1992) has advanced one form of instrumental stakeholder theory. Jones makes a theoretical case for the general proposition that if a project organization's contract (through their managers) with their stakeholders on the basis of mutual trust and co-operation, they will have advantage over organizations that do not. Put another way they will deliver and win future business. No assumption is made that managers will try to develop trusting and co-operative relationships with stakeholders, but an argument is made that if they do, competitive advantage will result.

As intimated in Section 1.1.2 many organizations have limited resources and as such stakeholders compete for these resources. Often as not stakeholder values and needs differ widely and there is usually a highly skewed distribution of resources among stakeholder groups. Typically on projects stakeholders have different priorities and different objectives. Unequal influence and distribution of resources exacerbate conflict of interests. For example, senior managers are normally part of the elite that have responsibility for and make the key decisions for the business direction of the project organization. Their role is to generally ensure that technology and information technology is integrated to the business processes of the organization, whereas employees the non-elite may be users of systems without any real influence. They are however, important stakeholders in the exploitation process because, in order to plan and implement software systems that can be efficient and integrated, their specific needs and requirements must be taken into account. However, they tend to fall into the underprivileged stakeholder category.

1.2.3 Gaining stakeholder commitment and trust

The importance of stakeholders during the software life cycle process is based on the premise that their activities in the development phases largely determine the quality of the finished product itself and as such stakeholders yield power and influence over the project manager (Schulmeyer and McManus, 1999). Research by McManus and Wood-Harper (2003) emphasises the need to gain stakeholder trust and commitment.

Project managers sometimes use their reputations to create trust with stakeholders. Reputation involves an estimation of ones character, skills and reliability, and other attributes important to the exchanges and is important under exchange conditions of uncertainty. As uncertainty within a project increases, exchanges between stakeholders become more focused with information about their own and others repudiation (Kollock, 1994). Reputation can reduce behavioural uncertainty by providing information about the reliability and good will of others. Reputations do have limitations in their use and so project managers must be able to legitimize their actions in the eyes of those stakeholders who are affected or who can affect the project's outcomes. In essence they need to establish credibility and engender trust.

It is relatively easy to tell when a project manager is behaving in ways that will reduce credibility and cause damage to the team or project. Trust-busting behaviours (or language) often kill hope of consensus or negotiation. This is not generally the fault of the stakeholders; but instead is strictly the failing of those who use this approach in the mistaken belief that it is effective or will somehow avoid having to deal with issues and questions.

McManus and Wood-Harper offer some strategic advice to the project manager looking to engender trust – their advice includes:

- establishing good personal relationships, expertise alone does not inspire trust and credibility
- illustrating that actions are being driven by the needs of the stakeholders, and that their needs and requirements are being considered seriously
- using the recommendations of stakeholders or established formal methodologies to support the project
- involving stakeholders as project champions to lend the project authority.

Mintzberg (1994) argues for caution when developing stakeholder strategies. He comments: *"Intended strategies have no value in and of themselves; they take on value only as committed people infuse them with energy ... that is why every problem of implementation is also one of formulation – not only for the actual strategies conceived but also for the process by which conceptualisation occurs"*.

In essence Mintzberg view is that managers should encourage active consultation and participation of as many stakeholders as possible, by engaging them in the ongoing dialogue, and involving them in the strategic process, to generate a feeling of consensus and ownership of the process and the outcomes throughout the organization. Stakeholders who have been consulted and have participated in the strategic process will better understand the trade-offs between project benefits and disadvantages and have greater trust. In this respect, stakeholder consultation can minimize the risk of unexpected negative reactions and protect and ensure a continued "licence to operate" and indirectly may lead to financial savings by avoiding social unrest, political or legal disputes, or negative publicity that can delay projects and be very costly. These aspects of software projects should not be forgotten. The project manager must be aware of the sensitive nature and issues of power and personal interests within the project or organization. The more high level and strategic a project is, the more such aspects have a vital importance on the success of the project. There is no clear recipe of what to do except to engage and consult stakeholders.

Boundaries of stakeholder consultation can be limited. For example, in Government or Health sector projects restrictions on resources or opportunities may act to curtail the involvement of the general public, leading to a reliance on key individuals or groups to represent stakeholder interests. However, organizations hoping to undertake a project involvement must realize that stakeholder consultation is just one component. Stakeholder processes are not public processes. If a company bases its actions on stakeholder consultation alone there is a possibility that the tax paying public will want to know why they were not consulted before a decision was reached and may even turn to the courts or officials to block decisions.

1.3 The principles of stakeholder management

I would like to discuss in more detail the seven principles of stakeholder management referred to in Figure 1.5 starting with principle number one.

Principle No. 1: Project managers have obligation to monitor the concerns of legitimate stakeholders and to take their interests into account.

In answering the question of what is a legitimate stakeholder? The first requirement of stakeholder management is an awareness of the existence of multiple and diverse stakeholders, and an understanding of their involvement and interest in the project. Many stakeholders are readily identified because of their express or implied contractual relationship to the organization. Others may identify themselves because of the impact, positive or negative, of the firm's activities on their own well-being. And, of course, some third parties may claim a *stake* in the firm when no such relationship, in fact, exists. Managers are not obligated to respond favourably to every request or criticism; they are, however, obligated to examine all such claims carefully before passing judgment on their validity.

The salience of specific stakeholder concerns varies among different areas of managerial decision-making, and according to the time horizon involved. Current working conditions are of greatest concern to employees; the cost and quality of products are of greatest concern to customers. Long-term survival and growth may be of greatest concern to investors and to the communities within which the firm operates. In taking particular decisions and actions, project managers should give primary consideration to the interests of those stakeholders who are most intimately and critically involved.

Principle No. 2: Project managers should keep an open mind when making decisions and activity involve stakeholders in the decision-making process.

Communication, both internal and external, is a critical function of project management, and effective communication involves receiving, as well as sending, messages. Hence, to understand stakeholder interests and to integrate various stakeholder groups into an effective wealth-producing team, managers must engage in dialogue. A commitment to engage in dialogue, however, does not constitute a commitment to collective decision-making: there are obvious limits as to the amount and content of information (particularly information about strategic options under consideration) that can be appropriately shared with particular stakeholder groups. Nevertheless, the more open managers can be about critical decisions and their consequences, and the more clearly managers understand and appreciate the perspectives and concerns of affected parties, the more likely it is that problematic situations can be satisfactorily resolved. Open communication and dialogue are, in themselves, stakeholder benefits, quite apart from their content or the conclusions reached.

Principle No. 3: Project managers should support processes and modes of behaviour that are sympathetic, sensitive, and respectful to stakeholders and their needs.

Stakeholder groups differ not only in their primary interests and concerns, but also in their size, complexity, and level of involvement with the corporation. Some groups are dealt with through formal, and even legally prescribed, mechanisms, such as collective bargaining agreements and shareowner meetings. Others are reached through advertising, public relations, or press releases; still others (e.g. government officials) are reached largely through official proceedings and personal contacts. Both the mode of contact and the type of information presented, or the opportunity for dialogue, can appropriately vary among different stakeholder groups, although the descriptions of situations and explanations of actions offered by managers should be consistent among all stakeholders. Extreme caution is required when project managers deal with stakeholder groups that have limited capacity to assimilate and evaluate complex situations and options.

Principle No. 4: Project managers should recognize the individual stakeholder sacrifices and take positive steps to ensure that any just risk reward strategy is implemented.

A firm's a purposive organization in which all voluntary stakeholders collaborate for mutual benefit. Involuntary or consequential stakeholders (e.g. communities or third parties) may also be affected by the operation of the enterprise. And both voluntary and involuntary stakeholders are vulnerable, and differently vulnerable, to the effects of uncertainty and change over time. Successful project managers will see that all stakeholders receive sufficient benefits to assure their continued collaboration in the enterprise, and that their burdens and risks are no greater than they are willing to bear. Again, the openness and demonstrable fairness of the distribution of benefits and burdens among stakeholders are, in themselves, stakeholder benefits. Project managers may need to make special efforts to demonstrate stakeholder interdependence and the collaborative nature of the enterprise to non-contractual and involuntary stakeholders.

Principle No. 5: Project managers should work to harmonize events that may destabilize stakeholder involvement.

Wealth creation necessarily gives rise to consequences that may not be fully mediated through the marketplace. Some of these may be beneficial and welcome; others may be harmful. Monitoring and ameliorating undesirable consequences (i.e. *negative externalities*) often requires co-operation with other firms, private sector organizations, public agencies, and units of government. Project managers should be proactive in developing contacts with relevant groups and in forging coalitions aimed at reducing harmful impacts and compensating affected parties.

The often-true observation that *one firm cannot solve this problem alone* should be a stimulus to multi-party co-operation, not an excuse for neglect and inaction.

Principle No. 6: Project managers should avoid activities that jeopardize human rights or give rise to risks that are unacceptable to stakeholders.

The ultimate consequences of most human endeavours (particularly endeavours involving large expenditures, diverse interests, and long-time periods) can never be fully anticipated in advance. Hence, managerial decisions and corporate operations necessarily give rise to multiple and diverse risks. Project managers should communicate openly with stakeholders concerning the risks involved with their specific roles in the corporate enterprise, and should negotiate appropriate risk-sharing (and benefit-sharing) contracts wherever possible. When stakeholders knowingly agree to accept a particular combination of risks and rewards, then the arrangement is usually considered satisfactory. However, some projects may have consequences for which no conceivable compensation would be adequate, or risks that cannot be fully understood or appreciated by critical stakeholders. In these circumstances, managers have a responsibility to restructure projects to eliminate the possibility of unacceptable consequences, or to abandon them entirely if necessary.

Principle No. 7: Managers have moral and legal responsibilities to stakeholders and should address conflicts through open communication.

Up to this point, we have spoken of project managers as if they were disinterested co-ordinators of stakeholder interactions. However, project managers also form a distinct stakeholder group, with privileged access to information and unique influence on corporate decisions. As stakeholders, project managers are naturally interested in the security of their jobs, the level of their rewards, and the scope of their discretion in the use of corporate resources. Other stakeholder groups (shareowners and boards of directors, in particular) have devised a variety of arrangements intended to align the interests of managers with those of the corporation as a whole, and to prevent opportunistic abuse of managerial positions. However, the tension between the interests of project managers as stakeholders, on one hand, and those of other stakeholder groups and of the corporation itself as an ongoing entity, on the other, is unavoidable. Responsible project managers will recognize this, and will therefore accept and encourage organizational practices intended to control this source of intra-organizational conflict. Project managers gain credibility when they establish procedures to monitor their own performance and, when appropriate, to facilitate third party review. Credibility matters when project managers ask other stakeholders to align their interests with those of the corporation, and to act responsibly rather than opportunistically. Without mutual credibility, stakeholder trust diminishes and the collaborative character of the organization may be jeopardized.

(Principles 1–7 are based on the work of Max Clarkson (Published by the Clarkson Centre for Business Ethics, Toronto, ON, 1999. ISBN 0-7727-8609-7 (paper). [59 pp.]) And are reproduced with permission.)

1.4 Key questions in stakeholder management

A number of the stakeholder issues have already been covered in Sections 1.1, 1.2, and 1.3. There are a number of key stakeholder questions that I would like to explore within this chapter. These questions relate to the what? Namely:

- What are our stakeholder's stakes?
- What challenges do the stakes and stakeholders present?
- What responsibilities does the organization have to stakeholders?
- What strategies should management adopt to manage its stakeholders?

1.4.1 What is a stake?

To appreciate the concept of stakeholders, it also helps to understand the idea of a stake. A stake can be described *as an interest or share in a project undertaking to achieve business, technical or social goals*. If we accept this broad definition, it must be asked, what are the stakeholder's interest, concerns, and perceptions of rights, expectations, or even ownership? As examples, consider two sets of stakeholders, the Organization and Government. The organizations interests are in maximizing profits, protecting intellectual property rights, balancing resource and demand, keeping the customer happy and other interests. The government's interest in an organization can be as regulators, tax collectors, customer of defence products, trade

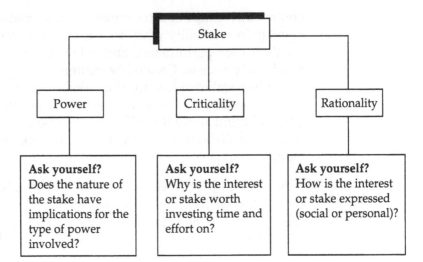

Figure 1.6
Defined components
of a stake.

balance manager, and many others related to the public good. In each of these cases, it is important to determine the power, criticality and rationality of each group with regard to each interest, Figure 1.6.

1.4.2 What challenges do the stakes and stakeholders present?

Challenges normally take the form of demands of or responses by the organizations. Challenges also arise when crises occur that appear to be the responsibility of business. For example, organizations engaged in the production of software systems sometimes face litigation for poor quality or late delivery. Another example is anti-trust cases, such as those recently publicized involving Microsoft. Where an organization accused of an anti-trust violation can face new challenges from government, customers, competitors, the media, the financial community, as well as others. A final example is software piracy where multiple stakeholders are affected.

The high rate of software piracy leads to more than just a loss of profit for companies. It also leads to a loss of jobs, wages, and tax revenue. In addition, companies have to charge higher prices for their software to account for their losses due to piracy. While it is easy to justify saving a few Euros by getting a piece of software for free, the impact on society as well as those around us must be considered. Each interest, of course, is of different degrees of importance.

1.4.3 What responsibilities does the organization have to stakeholders?

Mutual and joint responsibilities for stakeholders separate into two general categories or types of situation:

1. Between the organization and its stakeholders
2. Among stakeholders themselves

Organizations that make "demands" on stakeholders bear some responsibility of assurance that their "demands" do not generate unintended negative consequences for the stakeholder. Organizations and their project managers have both a moral and ethical duty to their stakeholders. If organizations and their project managers do not practice mutual respect they are presumably forced to turn to non-moral ways of dealing with moral conflict. In projects they are driven to count on procedural agreements, political deals, and threats – all of which obviously stand in the way of moral care. The underlying assumption is that organizations should value reaching conclusions through reason rather than force, and more specifically through moral reasoning rather than through self-interested bargaining. Nevertheless people holding such divergent moral values are still equal participants in a democratically structured decision process. Professor David Wong (Duke University, Durham, USA) has articulated principles for achieving this. Act on one's moral position in a way that minimizes potential damage to one's broader relationship to others who have opposed positions. Other things being equal, select issues that minimize opportunity for serious disagreement. In this case, we should decide policies on a fairly specific, rather than general level. A project-by-project framework is dictated by the nature of the diversity and complexity of the consequences of different proposed interventions. Organizations must adopt a willingness to bridge any differences. This permits domains of agreement to be ascertained by removing the "us vs. them" attitude. This is emphasized in organizations that promote internal value systems among stakeholders themselves.

1.4.4 Values among stakeholders

Based on practical experience I suggest that a stakeholder consensus would identify the following values as a minimum requirement for software engineering projects to be considered ethical:

- *The project manger should promote quality*. Quality includes technical variables such as the skills and knowledge of the professional but also that ethical issues are handled well and that compassionate and respectful attitudes are promoted and rewarded.

- *The project manager should promote equality.* All potential stakeholders should have an equal opportunity to access information.
- *The project manager should promote the independence of the project professional.* This is essential if the project manager is to perform the role of advocate. It is a prerequisite for the maintenance of trust.
- *The project manager should not contain perverse incentives.* Such incentives include those, which might encourage project managers to over service or to under service, and those, which might encourage stakeholders to make unreasonable demands on, project managers.
- *The project manager should promote professional accountability.* There should be no rights without responsibility, and conversely, there should be no responsibility without the right of professional autonomy.
- *The project manager should be able to reconcile conflicts between values.* The demand of stakeholder confidentiality and privacy, access to information to make informed choice, autonomous decision-making, and the values of stakeholders and those of the project manager are not always mutually compatible. Organizations should allow for the discretionary exercise of judgement.
- *The project manager should not make unreasonable demands on any of the stakeholders.* The requirement for equity of access to the service has been noted. However, software service providers should not be expected to provide services for which resources have not been provided.
- *The project manager should promote co-operation* rather than competition between service providers.
- *The project manager should promote continuity of service* and the exchange of values and beliefs over time.

1.4.5 What strategies should management adopt to manage its stakeholders?

After management has determined the responsibilities and stakeholders involved, a highly important question is, "What strategies should management adopt?"

In large projects where numerous stakeholders are involved it is perhaps true to acknowledge that it is highly unlikely that all stakeholders' expectations will be met. Therefore, the project manager must somehow ascertain which stakeholders should be satisfied. Since stakeholders have the ability to positively or negatively influence the project, integrating and satisfying the right people is essential. Specific organizational and project strategies used to integrate stakeholders will differ, depending on the issue and the groups potential to co-operate or threaten the organizations performance. In developing strategy, the project manager needs to consider that each stakeholder has the ability to both threaten and co-operate, the objective of the game is to reduce the threatening element and increase the co-operative behaviour of the stakeholder.

It is important to realize that the stakeholders potential to act and their willingness to act are not directly related. Therefore, when looking at strategies, it is important to examine not only strategies addressing stakeholders who are positively disposed towards a project but those who are negatively disposed towards a project as well. Some strategies may only be appropriate for a stakeholder with a specific disposition towards the project, that is, positive or negative. In other cases a given strategy may be appropriate for either type of stakeholder, that is both. Strategies should not be mutually exclusive; some are appropriate for more than one type of stakeholder.

This topic will be discussed in more detail in Chapter 5.

1.5 Chapter summary – 10 key points

The most important points to take away from this chapter are as follows. Remember:

1. Software projects need to follow a disciplined methodology
2. Selection of the right project manager with the right stuff is critical
3. Successful project managers recognize that many factors affect the outcome of a project
4. One characteristic a project manager must possess is the ability to see the big picture
5. Project managers should recognize dominant ideas that polarize perception of a problem
6. Creative and talented people matter
7. A stakeholder approach to project management will contribute to the long-term survival and success of a project
8. The bigger, the more complex the project, the more it is likely to involve a wider array of stakeholders

9. Project managers should support processes and modes of behaviour that are sympathetic, sensitive, and respectful to stakeholders and their needs

10. Credibility matters when project managers ask other stakeholders to align their interests with those of the project, and to act responsibly rather than opportunistically.

Chapter reading

Blumberg, M., and D. Gerwin (1981) Coping with Advanced Manufacturing Technology, International Institute for Management/Labour Policy, Berlin.

Davis, G.B. (1982) Strategies for information requirements determination. IBM Systems Journal, 21(1), 4–30.

Freeman, R.E. (1984) Strategic Management: A Stakeholder Approach. Boston, Massachusettts, Pitman Publishing Company.

Freeman, R.E. (1997) A stakeholder theory of the modern corporation. In Ethical Theory and Business. Beauchamp, T and Bowie, N (eds), Englewood Cliffs, NJ, Prentice-Hall, pp. 66–76.

Hill, C.W.L., and T.M. Jones (1992) Stakeholder-agency theory. Journal of Management Studies, 29, 131–154.

Kollock, P. (1994) The emergence of exchange structures: an experienced study of uncertainty, commitment and trust. American Journal of Sociology, 100, 313–345.

McManus, J., and T. Wood-Harper (2003) Information Systems Project Management, Chapter 2, UK, FT Prentice Hall.

Mintzberg, H. (1994) The Rise and Fall of Strategic Planning, Hemel Hempstead, UK, Prentice Hall International.

Mitchell, R., B. Agle, and D. Wood (1997) Toward a theory of stakeholder identification and salience: defining the principle of who and what really counts. Academy of Management Review, 22(4), 853–886.

Schulmeyer, G.G., and J.I. McManus (1999) The Handbook of Software Quality Assurance (3rd edition). Van Nostrand Reinhold Company.

Stakeholders within the Project Environment

2.1 The identification of stakeholders and their roles

In Section 1.2.1, it was noted that stakeholders are numerous and sometimes difficult to identify. What we do know is that stakeholder involvement is context specific; that is what works for one software project or situation may not be appropriate in another.

The broad view of stakeholder identification focuses on a stakeholder's ability to influence organizations behaviour, direction, process or outcome, and focuses on the urgency, power, and legitimacy of the stakeholder in question (see Mitchell *et al.*, 1997). However, because each type of stakeholder has a different legal, economic, and social relationship to a particular project, a general stakeholder identification approach may not be too helpful in defining and explaining specific obligations of managers to stakeholders.

2.1.1 Stakeholder analysis techniques

Stakeholder analysis helps project managers and their advisors to assess a project environment, and to inform the organizations negotiating position in project talks. More specifically, undertaking a stakeholder analysis will:

- draw out the interests of stakeholders in relation to the problems which the project is seeking to address or the purpose of the project
- identify conflicts of interests between stakeholders, which will influence the organizations assessment of a projects risks

before resources are committed (which is crucial for proposed projects)

- help to identify relations between stakeholders which can be built upon, and maybe enable coalitions of project sponsorship, ownership, and co-operation
- help to assess the appropriate type of participation by different stakeholders, at successive stages of the project life cycle.

As previously pointed out there are numerous approaches to stakeholder analysis, ranging from the formal to informal, comprehensive to superficial. The most common methods employed are:

1. QA checklists
2. mapping
3. tables (or matrixes)
4. peer and third-party reviews.

2.1.1.1 QA checklists

The checklist analysis method developed by the World Bank is a useful means to identify relevant project stakeholders. The World Bank guiding questions for identifying stakeholders include:

- Who might be affected (positively or negatively) by the development concern to be addressed?
- Who are the "voiceless" for whom special efforts may have to be made?
- Who are the representatives of those likely to be affected?
- Who is responsible for what is intended?
- Who is likely to mobilize for or against what is intended?
- Who can make what is intended more effective through their participation or less effective by their non-participation or outright opposition?
- Who can contribute financial and technical resources?
- Whose behaviour has to change for the effort to succeed?

The output from the analysis should generate information about stakeholders and their interests, the relationships between them, their motivations, and their ability to influence outcomes. The goal of stakeholder analysis is to:

- identify the stakeholders (by category)
- develop a strategic view of the situation, and the relationship between the different stakeholders and identified objectives

- guide the design of collaboration approaches, including the strengthening of existing positive relationships and the improvement of confrontational ones
- clarify stakeholder interests and roles (including one's own).

One difficulty with the World Bank model is that it is very much open to interpretation by the user to decide which questions to address first. It does however provide a good starting point for building up stakeholder profiles.

2.1.1.2 Mapping

The use of stakeholder maps was briefly discussed in Section 1.2.1 – this technique is widely used in stakeholder analysis and is an effective pictorial tool in explaining complex interstakeholder relationships.

One method of mapping was developed by William Trochim (of Cornell University, USA) and is known as *concept mapping*. The use and discussion of concept mapping as a tool in stakeholder analysis has been steadily growing over the past decade. Although several approaches to concept mapping have been developed, the approach detailed by Trochim (1989) is selected for discussion in the context of stakeholder mapping.

Trochim developed concept mapping as a type of structured *conceptualization*, which can be used by groups to develop a conceptual framework, which can guide evaluation or planning. In the typical case, six steps are involved:

1. Preparation (including selection of participants and development of focus for the conceptualization)
2. The generation of statements
3. The structuring of statements
4. The representation of statements in the form of a concept map (using multidimensional scaling and cluster analysis)
5. The interpretation of maps
6. The utilization of maps.

The stakeholder analysis approach must incorporate an appreciation that each project is likely to affect different stakeholder groups that have divergent and even incompatible concerns by realizing and legitimizing the diversity of interests at play. Inherent in this diversity, however, are problems of conceptual definition. According to Trochim conceptualization refers to the *articulation of thoughts, ideas, or hunches and the representation of*

31

these in some objective form. For example, during the planning phase of a project, we typically wish to conceptualize the major milestones, goals and objectives, needs, resources, and capabilities or other dimensions which eventually constitute the elements of a plan. On the other hand in evaluation, we may want to conceptualize the programmes or treatments, samples, settings, measures, and outcomes that we believe are relevant to the project.

In concept mapping, ideas are represented in the form of a picture or map. To construct the map, ideas first have to be described or generated, and the interrelationships between them articulated. Multivariate statistical techniques are then applied to this information and the results are depicted in map form. The content of the map is entirely determined by the group. They brainstorm the initial ideas, provide information about how these ideas are related, interpret the results of the analyses, and decide how the map is to be utilized and maintained (See Figure 2.1).

There are two major tasks that must be undertaken prior to commencement of the actual process. First, the project manager (or facilitator) must work with the parties involved to decide on

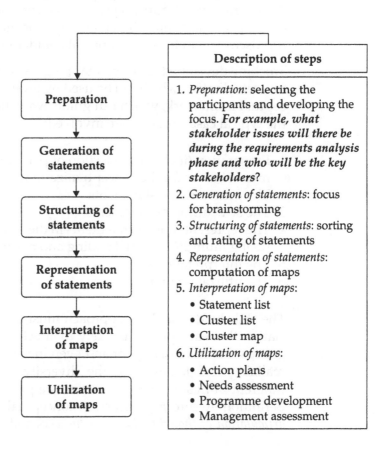

Figure 2.1
Concept mapping process for stakeholder analysis (after Trochim).

who will participate in the process. Second, the project manager must then work with the participants or a subgroup to decide on the specific focus for the conceptualization.

One of the most important tasks, which the project manager addresses, is who will participate in the mapping process. Trochim's experience has been that a conceptualization is best when it includes a wide variety of relevant people. If we are conducting a requirements planning exercise for a service organization, we might include administrative staff, service staff, board members, clients, and relevant members of community groups. In a project evaluation context, we might similarly include administrators, project staff, clients, community members, and relevant funding agent representatives. Broad heterogeneous participation helps to insure that a wide variety of viewpoints will be considered and encourages a broader range of people to "buy into" the conceptual framework results.

In summary there are many other ways to generate the conceptual domain than brainstorming. Sometimes a set of statements can be abstracted from existing text documents such as annual reports, internal organizational memos, interviews, or field notes.

Concept maps make good communicational tools. For example, graphics can represent information in a way that sometimes may be more appropriate to communicating both contents and an idea about the complexity of content. Concept maps are not limited by linearity and are convenient to represent what can be complex and intricate. Furthermore, they allow collaborative construction of knowledge.

This concept mapping process is by no means the only way in which group conceptualization can be accomplished nor is it necessarily the best way for any given situation. In situations where a group can achieve consensus relatively easily on their own or where a pictorial representation of their thinking is not desired or deemed useful, this approach would not be recommended.

(See Trochim, W. (1989) An introduction to concept mapping for planning and evaluation. In A Special Issue of Evaluation and Program Planning. Trochim, W. (ed.), 12(1), pp. 1–16.)

2.1.1.3 Tables (or matrixes)

Unlike concept mapping tables are a simple but effective means of identifying stakeholders without engaging too many resources. One mechanism to create this table is to use the project life cycle outlined in Figure 1.4, that divides the software engineering process into 12 stages, from requirements analysis, through design, coding, testing to implementation, and support. Using this life cycle as a basis, it is suggested that the project manager could adopt the following procedure to carry out this analysis exercise. Namely:

- Identify and list all potential stakeholders, using the template defined in Figure 2.2, the project manager identifies stakeholders to the project and inserts them on the *y*-axis of the matrix. It is left to the project manager to decide which stakeholders are involved in each stage of the project life cycle. This will obviously depend to some degree on the complexity of the project and the finance and procurement process used. For brevity, only a single stage is used in the example shown

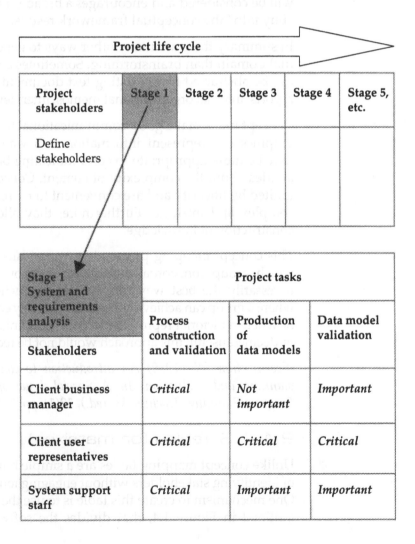

Project life cycle

Project stakeholders	Stage 1	Stage 2	Stage 3	Stage 4	Stage 5, etc.
Define stakeholders					

Stage 1 System and requirements analysis	Project tasks		
Stakeholders	Process construction and validation	Production of data models	Data model validation
Client business manager	*Critical*	*Not important*	*Important*
Client user representatives	*Critical*	*Critical*	*Critical*
System support staff	*Critical*	*Important*	*Important*

Figure 2.2
Example of stakeholder matrix.

in Figure 2.2. In reality, the exercise would be carried out for each of the 12 stages of the project life cycle.

- Identify stakeholder interests (or requirements (overt and hidden) in relation to the issues being addressed by the project and its objectives.
- Briefly assess the likely impact (risk) of the project on each of these interests (*critical, important, and not important*).
- Indicate the relative priority that the project should give to each stakeholder in meeting his or her interests (this refers to priorities derived from the project's objectives).

When using the matrix for your project, remember to use it as a set of general hints to help you discover the key roles and individuals playing those roles. Add table rows for additional stakeholders. Document stakeholders' actual names and their personal viewpoints on the project; if needed, document their roles in more detail, and record their job titles, departments, and other clues to their involvement on the project. Pay special attention to anomalies:

- If more than one stakeholder or group of stakeholders fills any positive role, there may be conflicting viewpoints on your project. Take care to discover the different viewpoints, and plan for conflict resolution workshops, or other preventative measures. For example, if the design role is split (design is split across more than one provider) then you must ensure there will not be constant debate on acceptance criteria, etc.
- If any role is unfilled on your project, there may be hidden requirements that will not be discovered until late in the project.
- If people are reluctant to discuss an area, this may be because it is known to be dangerous within the organization. Take care to understand the cause, and find out what kinds of risk it poses to your project.
- If some people say a role is important and some say it is not, this is always significant. Acknowledge the different viewpoints, remain neutral, and make clear that you are collecting viewpoints from all affected stakeholders.
- If you find the matrix does not exactly match the needs of your project – as is likely – then add roles or otherwise modify the template to reflect reality more accurately. It is suggested that the project manager undertakes the initial stakeholder assessment possibly with the senior design authority or technical architect (although do not rule out using other personnel such as account managers).

2.1.1.4 Peer and third-party reviews

Stakeholder analysis often involves sensitive and undiplomatic information. As suggested many interests are covert, and agendas are partially hidden. In such situations there will be few benefits in trying to uncover such agendas in public. To obtain a broad cross section of views some organizations prefer to undertake a mixture of assessments using peer and third-party reviews.

- *Peer assessment*: a party within the project team would assess an individual stakeholder. This could be as part of the project team selection process or as an assessment exercise on an established team.
- *Third-party assessment*: a trained assessor from an organization external to the project usually undertakes this initial analysis. This task is usually reserved for complex and high value projects where political interests are at stake.

Generally the role of third parties is to assist project managers in bringing stakeholders to the table, in communicating more effectively, and in reaching a mutually agreeable solution. They are particularly effective when a large number of parties are involved; the relationship between parties is contentious or unbalanced; and/or the issues are particularly complex. While third parties can play an important role in the collaboration process, it is important that they approach the process with neutrality and flexibility. Facilitated dialogue, regulated negotiations, or traditional mediation will not always work where the necessary level of participation by organizational structures, and political culture does not exist. Third parties (whether consultants or representatives from external agencies) can act as catalysts in these situations. Their presence can encourage the participation of community and project leaders, and of government or private sector representatives who might normally stand back from such a collaborative process. When these various representatives do come together, it is important to have trained facilitators available who can transform situations of potential mistrust and conflict into genuine consensus building.

When third parties are needed, it can be helpful to set up a small sub-team who will carry out the convening, mediation, or facilitation. Members of the team would bring important strengths to the task. Teaming a key member of the project team with an external stakeholder carries the benefit of potentially strengthening the project's capability.

(See for example the work of Margoluis, Richard, and N. Salafsk (1998) Measures of Success: Designing, Managing and Monitoring Conservation and Development Projects. Washington, DC, Island Press; Eade, D. (1997) Capacity Building: An Approach to People-Centered Development. Oxford, UK.)

2.1.2 Stakeholder roles

Clearly the identification of stakeholders is but one-half of the equation. The roles that stakeholder's plays are of equal importance. Project methodologies such as PRINCE2 provide benchmarks of role types in software projects. According to the requirements of each project, more than one person can share a role within the PRINCE2 structure, alternatively two or more roles can be combined.

2.1.2.1 PRINCE2 project roles

The PRINCE2 methodology defines responsibilities for project participants and promotes responsible communication among stakeholders. Responsibilities and duties are established at the outset of the project and provide for performance and management accountability. Management control of the project is ensured by formally assigning roles and responsibilities. The main roles in a software project are described as follows:

1. The customer
2. Project executive
3. Senior user
4. Senior supplier
5. Project manager
6. Team manager
7. Project assurance
8. Project assurance team
9. Business assurance co-ordinator
10. User assurance co-ordinator
11. Technical assurance co-ordinator
12. Project support
13. Configuration Librarian.

The roles within PRINCE2 are based on a *customer–supplier* environment where the customer wants the product or service and the supplier builds and provides it. Key roles of executive and senior user come from the customer organization. These combined with senior supplier (typically from the supplier

PRINCE2 role	Role description
1. The customer	The person or group who commissioned the work and will benefit from the end results
2. Project executive	Ultimately responsible for the project, must ensure the project gives value for money and balance the demands of business user and supplier
3. Senior user	Represents the users needs and expectations, ensuring these are met within the constraints of the business case
4. Senior supplier	Represents the business case for the supplier on the project board
5. Project manager	Responsible to ensure that the project produces the required products to the required quality standard they have the authority to run the project on a day-to-day basis and will usually come from the customer organization
6. Team manager	Team managers are responsible for producing certain products and managing a team of specialists to do it
7. Project assurance	Project assurance are responsible for undertaking independent reviews and monitoring the project for those members of the project board
8. Project assurance team (PAT)	Project assurance team incorporates the roles of PAT, BAC, and TAC
9. Business assurance co-ordinator (BAC)	PAT is responsible for monitoring the business case and report on anything that might affect it
10. User assurance co-ordinator (UAC)	UAC is responsible for monitoring the projects ability to deliver a product which meets the specification and quality requirements
11. Technical assurance co-ordinator (TAC)	TAC is responsible for undertaking and carrying out those assurance duties of the senior supplier
12. Project support	Provides advice on project management tools, guidance, and administrative services, can be referred to as project support office and include configuration management
13. Configuration librarian	Custodian and guardian of all master copies of the project's products, perhaps to also maintain the issue log for the project manager

Figure 2.3
PRINCE2 project roles.

organization but can be the in-house IT function) to form the three key roles within the project board.

The board commissions the project, receives progress reports and is responsible for the continuation of a PRINCE2 project through its stage boundaries. The project manager reports directly to the project board. The project assurance teams provide valuable assistance to the project manager as well as an independent view that gives the board greater confidence. Although a proprietary method, one of the benefits of adopting PRINCE2 is the emphasis it places on the role of users within the project organization. A brief overview of the 13 PRINCE2 roles is given in Figure 2.3.

2.2 The classification and characteristics of stakeholders

Once stakeholders are identified, they have to be characterized. As discussed above in order to characterize stakeholders, they need to be described, understood, and their roles and interaction need to be elaborated. In organizations that use traditional project management methods such as PRINCE2, stakeholders are normally defined as direct (*primary and secondary*) and indirect (*external and extended*). Those directly affected by a proposed project are clearly among the key stakeholders. They are the ones who stand to benefit or lose from the organizations operations or who warrant redress from any negative effects of such operations. It is these directly affected stakeholders, who are the most significant and occasionally the most difficult to identify and involve in participatory efforts. Although in traditional software projects they tend to be pulled from a narrow technical community and this restricted stakeholder community will reduce the likelihood that any relevant ethical issues are properly considered (a point we will address in Chapter 4).

Many individuals or institutions may be indirectly involved or affected because of their technical expertise or public and private interest in organizational policies or programs, or they may be linked in some way to those who are directly affected. Such stakeholders may include various intermediary or representative organizations, private sector businesses, and technical and professional bodies. For project managers identifying and enlisting the right intermediary groups can and does prove difficult at times and in some situations can turn out to be a process of trial and error.

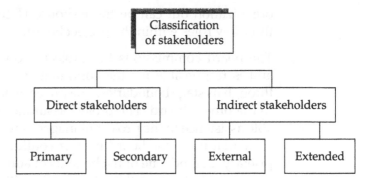

Figure 2.4
Stakeholder
classifications.

With primary, secondary, and external stakeholders there is a managing of interests; these stakeholders and their interests "must be dealt with" so that the project organization may achieve its goals. With extended stakeholders we seek some balancing of interests. Here, the stakeholder and ethics literatures intersect and gives a more bidirectional account of the project organization and its stakeholders. Figure 2.4 categorizes the types of stakeholders groups within a broad project community.

2.2.1 Primary stakeholders

Primary stakeholders include those who, because of power, authority, responsibilities, or claims over the resources, are central to any project initiative. As the outcome of any action will affect them directly, their participation is critical. Primary stakeholders can include private sector interests, and local and national government agencies.

This category of stakeholder also includes, by virtue of the power they wield, those who have *the capacity to influence collaboration outcomes*, but who may not themselves be directly affected by them. This group can include politicians and officials at the local, national, and regional levels, and international agencies who control policies, laws, or funding resources. Failure to involve primary stakeholders in collaboration efforts from the start can lead to subsequent implementation, technical, or political difficulties in achieving project objectives.

2.2.2 Secondary stakeholders

Secondary stakeholders are those with an indirect interest in the outcome. Depending on the issue, secondary stakeholders may, for example, be the consumer (who is interested in the continuing availability of a product or service), the company employee (who is concerned about job security). These stakeholders may need to be involved in collaboration processes, but their role may be peripheral to that of primary stakeholders, so they may need to be involved only periodically. Secondary stakeholders may need to have a role, for example, in identifying the costs and benefits of their interests or products, yet they may not need to be involved in all aspects of project initiatives. Project managers of collaboration projects need to plan when and how to include both primary and secondary stakeholders, as well as to monitor changes in their interests and influence.

2.2.3 External stakeholders

This third group of stakeholders by definition will be coming from outside the project community and will be expecting something from the project team. For the project manager it is necessary to recognize that what is added or exchanged for what is removed must be in proportion to the value of what has been removed, in essence the project manager must look towards external stakeholders adding value to the project in some way.

External stakeholders are likely to be groups recognized as impacting on a project but not being a direct part of the project team. In public sector sponsored projects among those included in the external stakeholders would be three important groups: government, regulatory agencies, and the treasury. In the case of national government, there would be the requirement that national activities be respectful of the needs and processes of local communities. Among other indicators, taxes could be used as a measurement of exchange between the local community and the national government, again with the measurement of balance being between the taxes paid and the services received in return.

It is perhaps worthwhile pointing out that because the commissioning of projects usually does not occur at the centre of construction; decisions have to be made regarding the distribution of the benefits, and costs that is:

- Where are the benefits to be made?
- Where will the costs of the projects accrue?
- How will the distribution of the benefits of the project affect the lives of the stakeholders and their communities?

Research undertaken by the *World Bank* on lessons on engagement has shown that it is critically important to adopt a step-by-step engagement of external stakeholders. This may require a commitment of time and resources to awareness raising, lobbying, advocacy, and building and nurturing mutual confidence. In working to introduce new ideas and approaches to governments and multilateral agencies at the international, regional, and national levels. Projects financed by the World Bank have used a variety of means to engage stakeholders. These techniques, including face-to-face discussions, the preparation and dissemination of policy and position papers, regular and persuasive correspondence, and the free provision of technical advice, were used to effectively allay actual and perceived government wariness of new concepts and proposals.

Project managers need to be aware that good ideas do not translate into action unless those with the power and influence to make change happen understand and support the common agenda. External stakeholders may often be helpful in assisting primary and secondary stakeholders to reach unified visions and develop realistic action plans that are feasible at administrative and political levels.

2.2.4 Extended stakeholders

There is no adequate definition to describe extended stakeholders a loose definition of this group is any individual that does not fit one of the previous three groups. For example, in NHS-related projects extended stakeholders tend to include patients, general public, opinion groups, or voluntary agencies.

2.3 The involvement of stakeholders in projects

One of the very first conversations that need to take place between the project manager and the stakeholders is how they view the issue, challenge, or opportunity that has brought them together. Strikingly different emphases can emerge from this discussion. For software design groups, the emphasis may be on how to conserve costs over the long term. For the customer, the emphasis may be on how to improve their working processes or preserve their culture. They may or may not view the project central to these goals. So too, different groups may in fact share similar views on the issue but express their objectives in different ways.

Any differences in perception and definition of the central goal and objectives need to be identified and addressed before the dialogue can move forward in a meaningful way. This is a key moment, as the stakeholders decide whose objectives will be at the heart of the venture, and whose will be less central. Next, the stakeholders must decide how to frame the central issues and tasks of a participation effort. Willingness to be flexible about how the overall task is framed will be key to securing the collaboration of a range of stakeholders. This negotiation towards participation can be expected to take some time. It may also result in some stakeholders opting out of the participation process.

Ray Jennings describes participation as:

> The involvement by a local population and, at times, additional stakeholders in the creation, content and conduct of a program or policy designed to change their lives. Built on a belief that citizens can be trusted to shape their own future, participatory development uses local decision-making and capacities to steer and define the nature of an intervention.

Alternatively, Shaeffer (1994) clarifies different degrees or levels of participation, and provides seven possible definitions of the term, including:

1. involvement through the mere use of a service (such as using a primary health care facility)
2. involvement through the contribution (or extraction) of money, materials, and labour
3. involvement through "attendance" (e.g. at meetings), implying passive acceptance of decisions made by others
4. involvement through consultation on a particular issue
5. participation in the delivery of a service, often as a partner with other actors
6. participation as implementers of delegated powers
7. participation "in real decision-making at every stage", including identification of problems, the study of feasibility, planning, implementation, and evaluation.

Shaeffer stresses that the first four definitions use the word involvement and signify largely *passive collaboration*, whereas the last three items use the word *participation* instead, implying a much more *active role*. Shaeffer further provides some specific activities that involve a high degree of participation in a wider development context, which can also be applied in the software development sector, including:

- collecting and analysing information
- defining priorities and setting goals

- assessing available resources
- deciding on and planning projects
- designing strategies to implement these programs and dividing responsibilities among participants
- managing projects
- monitoring progress of the programs
- evaluating results and impacts.

While many stakeholders may have the desire to participate in the project, they may lack the necessary capacity. Unless care is taken to communicate and negotiate on technical or political levels at which all stakeholders can engage, the broad collaboration processes required for many project settings will be precluded. As already noted, powerful stakeholders can end up controlling the process, particularly when activities are designed using the language and approaches that they develop. Therefore, an essential step in the participation process is determining the actual (or potential) capacity of stakeholders to participate actively and effectively in the process. The knowledge base, institutional and operational mechanisms, and skills of stakeholders are all capacities that the project manager should assess at the outset of the project. This assumes that participating groups agree to this. Being aware of a stakeholders strengths and weaknesses can inform the design and implementation of projects to help build the capacity of stakeholders to participate effectively in the collaboration process. It is clear that in order to be successful, all project stakeholders must actively work with your team to achieve these goals. There are several implications here:

1. Users, as indicated earlier, must be prepared to share business knowledge with the team and to make both pertinent and timely decisions regarding project scope and requirement priorities.
2. For senior managers to effectively support your project, they must first understand the technologies and techniques that your team is using, understand why your team is using them, and understand the implications of using them. With this knowledge, their efforts within your organization's political arena are far more likely to be effective at the right times and in the right ways. Senior managers won't be able to gain this requisite knowledge simply by reading a weekly project status report or by attending a monthly project steering meeting. Instead, they need to invest the necessary time to learn about the things that they manage. They need to actively participate in the development of your system.

3. Your operations and support organization must invest the resources required to understand both your system and the technologies that it uses. Your support staff must take the time to learn the nuances of your system, the implication being that they need to work with your system as it is developed and/or your team will need to provide them with training. Furthermore, your operations staff must become proficient with both the installation and operation of your system. You may choose to include one or two operations engineers on your development team or – once again – to invest project resources to train operations staff as required. Regardless of your approach, both your operations and support organizations will need to be actively involved with your project team.

4. Other project teams need to work with you if your system needs to integrate with other systems. For example, perhaps your system needs to access a legacy database, interact with an online system, work with a data file produced by an external system, or provide an XML data extract for other systems. Integration often proves difficult if not impossible without the active participation of these developers (imagine how difficult it would be to access the information contained in a large legacy database if the owners of that database refused to provide any information about that database).

5. Maintenance developers need to work with you to learn your system. When the intention is to either partially or completely hand off the maintenance of your system to other developers, it is common to bring in software professionals skilled in maintaining and enhancing existing systems to free up members of the original development team. Your team must work with these people so they can take over the system from you. Even when some original team members are still involved, an effort must be made to transfer the knowledge to the new members of the team.

(Points 1–5 are reproduced with permission of Scot W. Ambler, President of Ronin International, and are taken from Active Stakeholder Participation, May 2001.)

2.3.1 Forms of participation

Analysis of stakeholder types and their role in Section 2.1.2 clearly indicate that many project managers will describe participatory processes as the result of the interaction among a variety of primary, secondary, and external stakeholders. Each stakeholder brings into this interaction its particular interests and/or its mandate, which generates a continued negotiation on process objectives and procedures. Moreover, each stakeholder can play a variety of roles, according to a task sharing mechanism, which is itself the object of a continued trade-off. Based on the above, stakeholder participation tends to be described by key-informants as a highly *complex*, enthropic (i.e. disorder-prone) and idiosyncratic (i.e. case-specific and context-dependent) process. Thus, any valid conceptual and methodological framework for analysis and assessment of stakeholder participation should be flexible and open-ended enough to accommodate these (intrinsic) complexity, enthropy, and specificity.

Stakeholder involvement can take many forms. Practitioners and academics distinguish different dimensions, locations, degrees, and levels of participation in projects and programmes. These can refer to:

- Where in the project life cycle participation occurs. For example:
  - Pre-planning session
  - System requirements
  - Requirements analysis
  - Architecture design
  - Software development
  - Software testing
  - Implementation
  - Post-implementation reviews.

In essence participation can be interpreted along three broad lines (Oakley, 1991):

- Participation as contribution, that is voluntary or other forms of input by people to predetermined programmes and projects.
- Participation as organization, either externally conceived or emerging as a result of the process of participation.
- Participation as empowerment, enabling people to develop skills and abilities to become more self-reliant, and to make decisions and take actions essential to their development.

Participation in projects is widely seen as both a means and an end. While many project managers give equal weight to both, some emphasize one or the other aspect of participation. As an end, participation is seen as the empowerment of individuals and communities in terms of acquiring skills, knowledge, and experience, leading to greater self-reliance. Participation is an instrument to break people's exclusion and lack of access to and control over resources needed to sustain and improve their working lives. It is intended to empower them to take more control over their lives (Clayton *et al.*, 1998).

Another way of looking at forms of participation is a long, continuum of empowerment. In which stakeholders can be:

- *Beneficiaries*: recipients of services, resources, and development interventions through such things as community organizing, training, and one-way flow of information.
- *Clients*: capable of demanding and paying for goods and services from government and private sector agencies. For example, NHS-supported development projects focus more on building sustainable market-based financial systems, decentralizing authority and resources, and strengthening local institutions.
- *Owners and managers of their assets and activities*: the highest stage in terms of the intensity of participation involved.

Looked at from the perspective of any of the stakeholders in a project participation can include a range of possibilities:

- Being in control and only consulting, informing, or manipulating other stakeholders
- Partnership (i.e. equal powers of decision-making) with one or more of the other stakeholders
- Being consulted by other stakeholders who have more control
- Being informed by other stakeholders who have more control
- Being manipulated by other stakeholders (e.g. to contribute labour or money to an activity in which one has no interest or perceived benefit).

2.3.2 Benefits of participation

In the early 1990s the World Bank initiated an internal learning process on popular participation. The study included an international workshop in February 1992. The following presents a summary record of that workshop. Key benefits includes the following:

- More accurate and representative information about the needs, priorities, and capabilities of stakeholders as well as more reliable feedback on the impact of initiatives and programmes
- Adaptation or projects to meet local conditions so that scarce resources can be employed more efficiently
- Lower cost for services and financing

- Delivery of better quality and demand responsive services
- Mobilization of local resources to argument or even substitute scarce resources
- Improved utilization and maintenance of facilities and services
- Co-operation in new projects
- Increased recognition of achievements and legitimacy.

In recent times the trend towards collaborations and alliances have forced the providers of software services to move towards joint ventures where primary and external stakeholders have forged links to create sub-optimal projects without losing their flexibility or their roots in local culture. For example, small companies co-operating in networks are able to do the following:

- Share mounting costs (e.g. development and training).
- Access the expensive technologies they all need.
- Meld capabilities to produce sophisticated goods and services.
- Aggregate software processes to serve large customers and markets.
- The contribution to project planning, development, and implementation represent savings that reduce project costs.
- Learning from one another. They also contribute their knowledge of local conditions, facilitating the diagnosis of environmental, social, and institutional constraints, as well as the search for solutions.
- Increase market share.
- Given access to resources and a guarantee that they will share fully in the benefits of their efforts, they become more receptive to new technologies and services, and achieve higher levels of production and income. This helps to build net cash surpluses that strengthen the project groups' economic base.

2.3.3 Some pitfalls with participatory approaches

There are a number of potential pitfalls to take into consideration when engaging stakeholders. The first of these is that engaging secondary and extended stakeholders is often a far more difficult task than engaging the more powerful primary and external stakeholder groups. It is fairly easy to demonstrate to managers for instance why their participation in a particular initiative would be valuable. It is not the same for say the general public and therefore different techniques are required to achieve one's aim. For this reason, participatory approaches usually involve the project manager and the team working with and using those techniques described in Section 2.1.1.

Visual techniques are a good way to engage stakeholders especially where local staff are used in their preparation. Visual techniques also encourage creativity and the exchange of ideas. A second thing to bear in mind is that for participatory techniques to work effectively, the project manager must himself be prepared to change and learn to accept change if participation is to succeed.

2.4 Chapter summary – 10 key points

The most important points to take away from this chapter are given as follows. Remember:

1. the project manager needs to recognize that stakeholders have different legal, economic, and social relationships to a particular project
2. any stakeholder analysis must generate usable and definable information – realizing the diversity of interests at play within stakeholder groups
3. take care to discover the different viewpoints of stakeholders and plan for conflict resolution workshops or other preventative measures
4. the roles that stakeholders play are important. Responsibilities and duties should be established at the planning stage
5. do not underestimate the power stakeholders have (or acquire) during the life cycle of the project
6. differences in perception and definition of the central goal and project objectives should be addressed before any dialogue can move forward in a necessary manner
7. stakeholders sometimes lack the capacity to move the project forward
8. powerful stakeholders may end up controlling the project if communication takes a back-seat
9. participation in projects is widely seen as both a means and an end (but should not be seen as optional)
10. any conceptual framework for stakeholder participation must be flexible and open-ended enough to accommodate complexity and specificity.

Chapter reading

Clayton, A., P. Oakley, and B. Pratt (1998) Empowering People: A Guide to Participation. New York, UNDP.

Jennings, R. (2000) Participatory development as new paradigm: the transition of development professionalism. Prepared for the "Community Based Reintegration and Rehabilitation in Post-Conflict Settings" Conference. Washington, DC.

Mitchell, R., B. Agle, and D. Wood (1997) Toward a theory of stakeholder identification and salience: defining the principle of who and what really counts. Academy of Management Review, 22(4), 853–886.

Oakley, P. (1988) The Monitoring and Evaluation of Participation in Development. Rome, FAO.

Shaeffer, S. (ed.) (1994) Partnerships and Participation in Basic Education: A Series of Training Modules and Case Study Abstracts for Educational Planners and Mangers. Paris, UNESCO, International Institute for Educational Planning.

Trochim, W. (1989) An introduction to concept mapping for planning and evaluation. In A Special Issue of Evaluation and Program Planning. Trochim, W. (ed.), 12(1), pp. 1–16.

World Bank (1996) The World Bank Participation Sourcebook, Washington DC, The World Bank.

Capability and Stakeholder Management

3.1 Resources and issues management

Capability in project management is about providing products or services to customers that are fit for purpose and valued by the people that use them. With this objective in mind the discussion moves to whether the organization has the resources and competencies to provide the products and services that meet the customer and other stakeholder's requirements and expectations.

Resources required to deliver software projects will typically come from within and outside the organization. Allocation of resources is often seen as a major source of conflict between stakeholder groups. For example, the inability to provide suitable technical personnel and users during system and user acceptance testing (UAT) has been a longstanding issue with many project managers. To emphasis this point take the following statement made by one (anonymous) project manger:

> ... it seems to me one of the enduring problems in the organization on these issues has been that, although there are a large number of very talented people in the organization, I do not think it has had a sufficient depth of expertise on the very complicated range of technical issues, operational issues, and market issues which are required to see the project through to a satisfactory and timely conclusion.

As pointed out in Section 2.3.1 during the initial pre-planning sessions the project manager should develop a threshold level of resources required to deliver each stage of the project. This of course should not be carried out in isolation and should include the client and as many key stakeholders as practically possible. Why? Clearly some organizations may not be able to resource the project and meet the threshold requirements of its customers. This occurs not only because resources dissipate or skills become obsolete but, more importantly, because of competing projects and competing demand.

A study undertaken by Baker *et al.* on 650 projects in the US highlighted a number of key stakeholder issues that contributed to the success of a project. These key issues identified are:

- project commitment (to established schedules, budget, and performance)
- frequent feedback from the client organization
- frequent feedback from the customer
- customer commitment (to established schedules, budget, and performance)
- organization structure suited to the project team
- customer and client enthusiasm
- client desire to build internal capabilities
- adequate control procedures, especially for dealing with changes
- judicious use of networking techniques
- minimal number of public and government agencies involved
- reduced use of red tape
- enthusiastic public support
- lack of legal encumbrances.

In contrast Ferry and Brandon relate time, cost, and quality requirements to contractual arrangements. Time requirements range from no critical requirement and early completion to shortest time and earliest start. Reliable guaranteed completion dates and provision for phased completions are also included as needs. Cost requirements follow a similar format and also include low maintenance costs, balance between capital and maintenance costs, cash flow, share in the risk of development, and minimum capital commitment. Thus predictability of cost and time, lowest cost, and shortest time for stages of the project are regarded as different objectives applicable to different clients and projects.

In 2001, I sent e-mail correspondence to 20 of my fellow project managers (all responded) asking them to define their top stakeholder and project issues. Their responses are summarized in Figure 3.1.

Based on their answers it is clear that the successful completion of any project requires input from a variety of stakeholder

Key issue area and statement	Score (%)
Capability to deliver	
Determining whether the organization as the capability to deliver – see Section 3.2	100
Funding and contracting	
Determining who pays for changes in requirements	65
Determining who funds additional resources	25
Enforcing the contract	10
Roles and responsibilities	
Determining who has the responsibility for role allocation	35
Determining who has responsibility for accepting plans	25
Continuity of roles and involvement	25
Defining role of project board	10
Defining the role of external stakeholders	5
Technology and planning	
Determining the appropriate methodology	30
Determining and agreeing the plan	20
Reducing technical risk	20
Meeting client schedules	15
Determining equipment availability	15
Training	
Determining training needs to address different stakeholder needs	60
Determining who pays for *ad hoc* or unplanned training	30
Determining the right expertise	10

Figure 3.1
Key stakeholder
and project issues
(2001).

groups. Each stakeholder has a role in defining and determining success. Going back to our PRINCE2 roles in Figure 2.3, each actor has specific responsibilities that must be fulfilled in order to achieve success. The senior user for example, is expected to represent the users needs and expectations, ensuring these are meet within the constraints of the business case. Projects are normally instigated at the request of the customer, and the financial and other benefits for the customer and their stakeholder's hinge on its successful implementation. Customers can and should not expect to abdicate responsibility by passing all the duties to the project team.

The project team will be oriented towards objectives, which are only a subset of the overall aims of a project. The customer must ensure that an emphasis on the subset does not threaten the achievement of the wider aims from which it is drawn. Facilitating the team is important for the customer but, in the final analysis, the project is not instigated to facilitate the team. The project originates from a requirement to meet a need that exists for the customer and its stakeholders. That initial need must be kept in focus by all those stakeholder involved in the project.

3.2 Capability vs. competence

Competency is defined as the collective know-how of an organization that gives it a competitive advantage. This know-how is a result of learning that is driven by business strategy and built through a process of continuous improvement and enhancement that may span a decade or longer. (Grady, Successful Software Process Improvement, p. 39). Put another way competency is created when resources (internal and external) are deployed into those activities associated with delivering products and services. Competency is about the activities of an organization (*or in our case projects*) and the processes that link activities together both within and beyond the organization. Usually the key to good or poor performance is found here rather than in the resources *per se*.

Although an organization will need to reach a threshold level of competence in all activities it undertakes, only some of these activities will be regarded as core to a particular project undertaking. Core competencies should not be seen as being fixed. Core competencies usually change in response to changes in the company's environment. They are flexible and evolve over time. As a project evolves and adapts to new circumstances and opportunities, so its core competencies will have to adapt and change. See examples in Figure 3.2.

3.2.1 Capability maturity models

The impetus of software organizations to use capability models such as *People-Capability Maturity Model* (P-CMM) to assess and measure their software and people processes have proven beneficial when assessing threshold levels for competency and stakeholder management.

Software organization competence	Software project manager competence
Use of mature processes (and continuous improvement methods)	Creative problem solver (good rapid memory)
Ability to deliver complex software engineering projects	Ability to deal with complex issues (or abstractions)
Project management	Ability to communicate at all levels
Ability to undertake and invest in research and development	Ability to organize self and others
Ability to react quickly to market demands	Good all-round technical knowledge of subject discipline

Figure 3.2
Comparative examples of competencies.

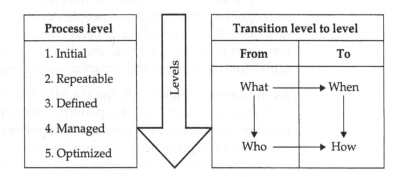

Figure 3.3
P-CMM overview model.

P-CMM is a conceptual model, but at the same time it has all of the necessary qualities of any other models (previously described). It is generalized, it represents major aspects of the software development process that are appropriate to the associated problems; and it has the capability to define the behaviour of the organization. Figure 3.3 defines the basic model. I would now like to focus on the characteristics of P-CMM.

P-CMM centres on the people component and provides a framework by which any organization can measure its people activities. The objectives of P-CMM are to:

- improve the capability of the people
- ensure that software development capability is an attribute of the organization
- align the motivation of individuals with that of the organization.

P-CMM describes an evolutionary improvement path from *ad hoc*, inconsistently performed activities, and working practices, to a matured and disciplined, and continuously improving development of the knowledge and skills and motivation of the workforce. In essence the P-CMM helps software project organizations (and their project managers) in the following ways:

- Characterize the maturity of their workforce
- Guide a programme of continuous workforce development
- Set priorities for immediate actions
- Integrate workforce development with process improvement
- Establish a culture of excellence.

The benefit of P-CMM is in narrowing the scope of activities to those practices that provide the next foundation layer for a project organization's continued people development. The practices described in Figure 3.4 have been chosen from industrial and service experiences as those that have a significant impact on individual, team, unit and organizational performance.

As indicated in Figure 3.3, the P-CMM has five levels. Level 1 represents a general lack of capability, the organization typically provides forms for activities such as performance appraisals, but offers little guidance or training in conducting the activities supported by the forms. In the worst circumstances, managers in level 1 organizations do not accept developing staff under their immediate control as primary personnel responsibility. Individuals in most level 1 organizations do not take practices seriously, since they do not believe the practices have much relation to their real work and level of contribution.

Level 2	Level 3	Level 4	Level 5
Repeatable	Defined	Managed	Optimizing
Working Environment Communication Staffing Performance management Training Compensation	Knowledge and skills analysis Workforce planning Competency development Career development Competency-based practices Participatory culture	Mentoring Team building Team-based practices Organization competency management Organizational performance alignment	Personal competency Development Coaching Continuous workforce innovation

Figure 3.4 P-CMM framework (McManus, 1999).

For each level above 1, there is a set of process areas that have to be mastered. Each process area maintains a match between two important elements of people management, for example work environment and performance. These process areas connect to form a network, which only becomes complete when level 5 is reached. A fundamental premise underlying the framework is that a practice cannot be improved if it cannot be repeated. Level 2 is primarily focused on assisting project organizations, remove the impediments that keep them from improving. A number of improvement themes run through the P-CMM. These themes help organize an understanding of the structure of the model and the relationships among key process areas.

3.2.1.1 Maturity levels

The repeatable: level 2
The key process areas for level 2, repeatable, aim to eliminate problems that keep people from being able to perform their work (and project) responsibilities effectively and to establish a foundation of practices that can be continuously improved. The most frequent problems that keep people from being able to perform effectively in low maturity project organizations include:

- environmental distractions
- unclear objectives
- lack of relevant knowledge and skills
- poor communication.

In maturing to the repeatable level, an organization establishes policies that commit it to developing people.

The defined: level 3
At the defined level the project organization begins to adopt its workforce practices to the specific nature of its business. By analysing the skills required by its workforce and business functions they perform, the organization identifies the core competencies required to perform its business activities. In essence a programme is defined for systematically developing core competencies, and individual career development strategies are planned to support competency development for each individual. The idea being that the organization administers its workforce practices to develop and reward growth in its core competencies and apply them to improve performance.

The managed: level 4

At this level, the project organization takes its first steps in capitalizing on managing its core competencies. It sets quantitative objectives for growth in core competencies and for alignment of performance across the individual, team, unit, and other organization levels. These measures establish the quantitative foundation for evaluating trends in the capability of the workforce. Further, it seeks to maximize the effectiveness of applying these competencies by developing teams that integrate complementary knowledge and skills. Trend information is used to evaluate the effectiveness of competency-related practices. Performance data is collected and analysed for trends in the alignment of performance at the individual and team levels. Trends in the alignment of performance are used to evaluate the effectiveness of performance-related work practices. These trends should be tracked against the strategic objectives of project organization. In theory the capability of a level 4 organization is predictable because current capability of the workforce is known quantitatively. The organization should have developed a mechanism for deploying competencies effectively through high-performance, competency-based teams.

The optimizing: level 5

At this level, there is a continuous focus on improving individual competencies and finding innovative ways to improve motivation and capability. The organization supports individuals' effort towards continuous developments of personnel competencies. Mentors should be provided to support team members. In essence improvement happens both by incremental advancements in their existing practices, and by adoption of innovative practices and methods that may have a dramatic impact (Figures 3.5 and 3.6).

3.2.1.2 P-CMM benefits

In order for the improvement to be deemed successful, an organization has to take pride in the implementation of the improvements and the results have to be seen and accepted. Improvements are one-time achievements, but pride feeds on itself and leads to continuous measurable improvement. When the whole organization buys into the improvement and sees the results unfold, it gains a team *esprit de corps* and from that, pride. Those organizations (in the US) that have embarked on implementing the P-CMM framework report considerable tangible and non-tangible benefits. I have summarized the main benefits in Figure 3.7.

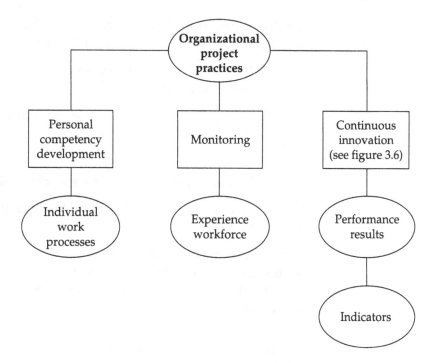

Figure 3.5
Optimizing model
(McManus, 1999).

Process area	Match between	Positive indicators	Negative indicators
Continuous innovation	Performance results	Systematic evaluation of innovative practices and technologies	Isolated pockets of innovation – lack of dissemination
		Empowerment to improve activities (individual and team)	Inertia in workforce practices

Figure 3.6
Optimizing
decomposed.

1. Reduction in labour turnover	6. Improved internal standards
2. Reduction in software production/ rejection rates	7. Improved internal relationships
3. Reduction in end-to-end process time	8. Improved focus on employee training needs
4. Reduction in software delivery cycles	9. Improved ergonomic/ working conditions
5. Improved company awareness	10. Improved employee reward systems

Figure 3.7
P-CMM benefits.

(See Humphrey, W.S., T.R. Snyder, and R.R. Willis. Software Process Improvement at Hughes Aircraft. IEEE Software, pp. 11–23.)

(Source: McManus, J. (1999) Climbing the Maturity Ladder, Part 1. Project Management Today, pp. 30–31.)

Note: Capability Maturity Model (CMM) is a registered trademark in the US Patent and Trademark Office.

3.2.2 Capability and task definition

Like brother and sister, capability and task definition are related to each other.

Task definition is what a person does on the job when carrying out his or her responsibilities. Project managers will, for example, have to demonstrate specific behaviours including but not limited to:

- makes judgements/decisions
- interacts with others
- provides services
- produces a product
- evaluates (people, products, programmes, and events)
- makes judgements plans (activities, programmes, etc.)
- implements (activities, programmes, etc.).

Tasks should be linked to common project goals and milestones and usually manifest themselves in project and milestone plans. Project size plays an important role here, and influences the way resources are allocated to the project (Figure 3.8).

Task definition is clearly linked to a number of project critical success factors (CSF). These include:

- workload allocations
- project performance
- individual performance
- schedule changes
- time control
- cost control
- project reviews.

Within project management CSF are undoubtedly linked to measurement and control systems within project management

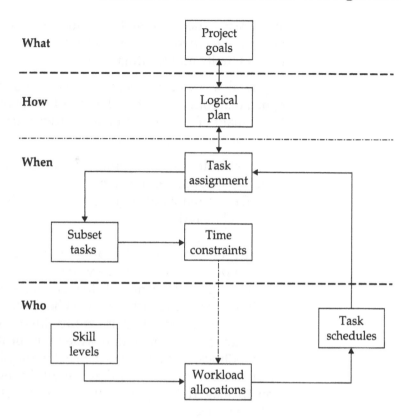

Figure 3.8 Plans to task model.

(a point we will come back to later in Chapter 6) and here the focus is on:

- What you are being asked to do?
- How will you be evaluated for process and product?
- What must you do to complete the task and finish the product?
- What should you do to get started?

3.3 Defining stakeholder commitment

In Section 1.2.3 we discussed in part the importance of gaining stakeholder commitment. The literature dealing with commitment has mainly been interested in aspects related to individual level commitment. However, rather that focusing on a single software occupation, software projects generally concern groups of professionals such as designers or even an organization as a whole. Software-related commitment research has acknowledged the existence of multiple level commitments. It is however, difficult to provide a clear-cut definition of commitment due to the existence of different interpretations. In commitment research, the term commitment is broadly used to refer to past history and consequences, as well as to the process of becoming committed or attached, or to the state of commitment or attachment itself (O'Reilly and Chatman, 1986).

Empirical work undertaken by Newman and Sabherwal have argued that commitment on the part of stakeholders is a necessary determinant of the success of any software project or component of the software project life cycle.

For a project to succeed, commitment must come from all levels of the organization and be persistent throughout the project life cycle. Determinants of commitment according to Newman and Sabherwal include:

1. project determinants that are objective attributes associated with a project such as cost and return on investment
2. psychological determinants that are the relationships that key individuals and decision-makers have with the project
3. social determinants that are groups involved with the project, the public, or organization-wide identification with the project, politics, and prior resistance that may have existed
4. structural determinants that are attributes such as political and managerial support for the project, the strategic positioning of the project.

These four levels also identify actors capable of showing commitment towards a certain commitment target.

Newman and Sabherwal (1996) describe a dynamic model of commitment that recognizes the volatility of systems projects. This model includes the stages of making the initial commitment, withdrawing the commitment, committing to a new approach, and the ensuing events including systems development activities. The initial commitment phase is influenced by the project determinants of budget, cost, and anticipated benefits. As the project evolves, social and structural determinants (key project relationships, public identification with the project) may decline leading to the withdrawal of commitment. After this withdrawal, the organization will again become aware of the problematic factors that were the original impetus for the project and the psychological determinants (i.e. key decision-makers) will reassert themselves and renew the project determinants resulting in an escalation of commitment.

System projects, particularly those involving enterprise systems, are very long term. According to Newman and Sabherwal, it is easier to maintain commitment if problems experienced during a project can be attributed to temporary causes or specific, avoidable project features. If an organization perceives a problem to be chronic and without resolution, commitment will fade. The long-term nature of information system projects can also impact the continuity of the project team, which is often the project's core commitment source. To address this, system development projects should be supported by a wide group of stakeholders to ensure continuity even if the project champion or key team members leave.

(The paragraph describing the Newman and Sabherwal dynamic model of commitment is based on determinants of commitment to information systems development: a longitudinal investigation. MIS Quarterly, 20, 23–54.)

3.4 Defining stakeholder interests

Clearly successful development of a project is dependent upon stakeholder commitment. As discussed commitment is a complex state involving the external forces imposed upon the individual or organization, and the element of time that may or may not correspond to the timeline of the project. This said another implication for project management is the "proposed view" of stakeholder and management interests as that of a dominant coalition of actors that changes over time, subject to many influences. This combined with the idea of mutual influence and co-dependency in the control relationship suggests a need to place considerable emphasis on communication, relationship building, and influence.

During the identification stage (Chapter 2), stakeholders will have been identified and listed in a table with their key project roles (see Figure 2.2). In identifying stakeholder interests the key is to keep in mind that identifying interests is done with stakeholders' perspective in mind, not your own. This is difficult as interests are usually hidden and may contradict openly stated aims. Each interest should be related to the appropriate project stage; that is, interests change as the project moves from beginning to ending phases. With some stakeholders it may be crucial to extract interests by formally asking them questions such as:

- Whose interests should be served?
- Who should benefit?
- What are the stakeholder's expectations of the project?
- How does the stakeholder regard other stakeholders?

I would like to discuss the first question in this section the remaining questions will be discussed in Chapter 4. In deciding whose interests should be served an example will be used. The example is based on the Australian General Practice Computing Advisory Group (AGPCG) Accreditation Feasibility Project.

3.4.1 Accreditation feasibility project interests

The Department of Health and Ageing, in partnership with the General Practice Computing Group (GPCG), sought to conduct a feasibility study into establishing a software supplier accreditation process across the health sector.

The accreditation scheme would address the major concerns raised by general practitioners (GPs) relating to the software that they use. Concerns identified include problems with transferring data from one software package to another, difficulty in entering data, poor data extraction, problems around software upgrades, and difficulties with the reliability of software support services.

The aim of potential health software supplier accreditation process would be to identify software suppliers with appropriate software development processes, raise the standards of software packages in the health sector and increase users and consumers confidence in the quality and reliability of software supplied to the health industry.

The range of stakeholders involved in the project covered government, consumers, industry, wider health professionals, and the supplier. Figure 3.9 identifies some stakeholder interests.

Once the major interests are identified, it is also useful to outline how the project will be impacted if these interests are or are not met. In most cases, a simple annotation of positive, negative, or unknown can be used as well as high, medium, low, or uncertain. To align project success criteria with interests, an additional step is to give a rough prioritization of each stakeholder with their accompanying interests. Since not all needs can be met with the same level of intensity or at the same time, a prioritization schema would be beneficial. Figure 3.10 provides an example of this information.

(See for example Cleland, D. (ed.), (1998) Field Guide to Project Management, John Wiley and Sons.)

Stakeholder	Major interest	Need to know
Supplier	Delivery of project Repeat business Profits Public image	Risks Political climate Future business potential Business climate
Sponsor	Costs to deliver project Methods of delivery Impact on future budgets Impact of resources	Risks Impact on process Impact on other stakeholders
GPs	Implications on their practice: • Time implications • Cost implications • Staff and training	Time scales Resource implications
Government	Public image Policy implications Implementation costs	Cost of failure Damage to service

Figure 3.9
Examples of major
stakeholder
interests.

Stakeholder	Major interest	Need to know	Impact	Priorities
Supplier	Delivery of project	Risks involved	+High	3
	Repeat business	Political climate	+High	3
	Profits	Future business potential	+High	3
	Public image	Business climate	+High	3

Figure 3.10
Examples of
stakeholder
interest and
impact.

3.5 Defining stakeholder power

The majority of projects are not self-contained or self-sufficient, stakeholder groups must be relied upon to provide support for the project. For continuing to provide what the project needs, stakeholders may demand certain *quid pro quos* from the project manager in return. In short, it is the dependence of the project on stakeholders (particularly external stakeholders) for favours (and resources) that give those individuals involved leverage over a project. In applying this leverage, power and influence plays a large part. Power can be defined as: *the structural determined potential for obtaining favoured payoffs in relations where interests are opposed* (Willer *et al.*, 1997). Alternatively Moss Kanter (1985) describes power as *the ability to get things done.* Although such a definition is straightforward, it has significant appeal in relation to the role of project managers. It is particularly helpful since much of the skill of a project manager revolves around the ability to manage the political power dimensions within and around the stakeholder community, so much so that failure to understand and control the political process has been the downfall of many good managers. Within the stakeholder community politics is concerned with the way in which managers gain and use power and involves them in a range of activities, such as bargaining for resources striking deals, forming coalitions with others, and so on (McManus and Wood-Harper, 2003). Clearly it is important for project managers to have above average political skills in order to gain and keep power. Nico Machiavelli for example, *advised political leaders on how to acquire power, resist dissent, and control sub-ordinates. Machiavelli's cynical view of his fellow man is best summed up by his comment "Men are in general ungrateful, fickle, false, cowardly, jealous, but as long as you succeed, they are yours entirely".* It could be argued that when power is at stake, questions of morality are irrelevant and that lying, deceit and manipulation are all legitimate tactics.

From an individual stakeholder perspective, winning the game by whatever means (power or influence) is all that matters. Power, however, is relative in the sense that the source of the project manager's power lies not in himself, but in his followers. In essence the project manager can only exercise the power, which his followers allow. Social and behavioural researchers (Clegg, 1997) have identified several frameworks of power. Definitions of power include many levels of analysis. French and Raven (1959) argue that individual stakeholders accumulate power from the following bases: reward, coercive, expert, legitimate, and referent power. For project managers the acquisition of political power for example stems from being supported by a stakeholder group. To gain power the project manager must be able to work with powerful stakeholders so that he can gain allegiance from them. The exercise of power and influence leads to direct and indirect consequences for both the stakeholder and the project manager. As the complementarity hypothesis suggests, coercive, powerful influence tactics often lead to submissive, passive reactions in the target. Such methods, however, usually generate compliance rather than identification or internalization. These latter two reactions are more likely when rational methods of influence are used. For example, project managers who use coercive methods on stakeholders normally experience dysfunctional group feedback, including: dislike and rejection, anger and reciprocal conflict, revolutionary coalitions, reactance, reductions in intrinsic motivation, and self-blame.

As previously stated project managers are often seen by stakeholders as experts in their field and as such can yield expert power. Expert power stems from the project manager having the knowledge and skill in an area the stakeholder does not (usually technical); therefore in this area the stakeholder is usually willing to accept the project manager's advice. Project managers look to obtain the stakeholder's allegiance through persuasion. Expert power in an area, which is crucial to the attainment of the organizations success, may give the project manager an important organizational role with its associated position power source. So if the project manager's expertise is questioned it may be possible for the project manager to resort to the methods associated with legitimate power.

The role and duties of differing stakeholders can, of course, conflict with differing power interests. This aspect is particularly important, because it can help explain the actions and reactions of differing project contributors. The tension between official project roles and duties, and personal interests are important. Various sources of intra- and interpersonal conflicts can be identified, for example, the project may have a single contributor that is assigned several roles with conflicting goals and duties; a single stakeholder can be assigned roles with goals and duties which conflict with personal interests; and a single contributor may be assigned roles and goals and duties which conflict with goals and duties of other stakeholders. Clearly what is required is demarcation of power and responsibilities.

Kipnis (1976) in his studies of the metamorphic effects of power find that people who are given coercive power will use this power and that once it is used, the power holders tend to overestimate their control over others and devalue these targets. Power holders who are very secure in this position may also overstep the bounds of their authority in a process termed the mandate phenomenon, or they may become so besotted with power that they are pre-occupied with gaining it and using it for their own ends. We will return to this subject again in Chapter 4.

3.6 Predicting stakeholder problems

Conflict and power interests are clearly related and not to loose the essence of the importance of conflict and conflict situations I would like to shift the discussion to predicting stakeholder problems to reduce the probability of conflict situations occurring. In software engineering projects there are many pitfalls to successful delivery and as stated in Chapter 1, many of these problems arise from poor planning and lack of stakeholder involvement during the early stages of the project. In predicting what stakeholder problems may arise the project manager is advised to focus on lessons learned from previous projects. For example, traditionally, requirements engineering receives a relatively small percentage of project resources throughout the project life cycle. A review by McManus (2004) of 58 previous project lesson learned reports found the following key problems during the requirements engineering stage:

- Inadequate customer involvement.
- Poorly delimited scope of systems.
- Constantly changing requirements due to factors beyond the control of the stakeholders.
- Vague and ambiguous requirements.
- Requirements presented without prioritization.
- Requesting functionality no one uses.
- Allowing the requirements to change without configuration control.
- Not addressing all requirement categories.
- Requirements are expressed in the language of the application domain, which may not be understood by software engineers, developing the system.
- Domain specialists understand the area so well that they do not think of making the domain requirements explicit.
- Stakeholders do not know what they really want.
- Stakeholders express requirements in their own terms.
- Different stakeholders may have conflicting requirements.
- Organizational and political factors may influence the system requirements.
- The requirements change during the analysis process. New stakeholders may emerge and the business environment change.
- Language. Often, in the public sector, requirements are developed in one of the three common methodologies. It is not always possible to have all stakeholders agree on which methodologies to use.
- Writing implementation (*how*) instead of requirements (*what*).
- Over-specifying.

Most of the projects reviewed had requirements with multiple stakeholders. About a third of the projects performed walkthroughs to verify and validate requirements with their sponsors. Although two-thirds did not – the writers in summing up emphasized the importance of including customers and users in peer reviews and walkthroughs (See also Chapter 6).

3.6.1 Problem management

All lesson learned reports are of course dealing with retrospective issues and they are in essence to do with cause and effect. The central principle behind the activities of any project is that every effect (every change) is the result of a cause. This might sound painfully obvious, but it is also the part of investigation that is so obvious that it is frequently forgotten by the inexperienced. The art of making an investigation, as Sherlock Holmes knew, is to build a chain (sometimes a more complicated web) connecting the observed evidence with a proposed theory. Until this is done, any "explanation" of an occurrence is simply speculation, or assertion.

In predicting stakeholder problems the project manager "must" be able to recognize whether a problem exists, be able to identify the components of the problem and create a plan of action to resolve the problem. The challenge during problem selection is to move from a generalized issue to a focused problem that can be acted on. If we develop and implement plans based only on a general understanding of a broad issue, we run the risk of underestimating the complexity of the issue and the results we can achieve will be limited.

In Section 1.1 we briefly touched on the use of lateral thinking (*see De Bono Chapter 1 reading*). Most seasoned project managers whether consciously or subconsciously use lateral thinking and other cognitive approaches when faced with complex issues and problems. Although our previous example was linked to requirements engineering many stakeholder problems tend to be associated with non-technical issues and involve people from other stakeholder groups.

Edward De Bono's critical thinking "*six hats*" method is a good approach to scenario building and provides the project manager with a critical thinking tool for stakeholder problem solving. The six hats promotes and facilitates structure and efficiency, and helps significantly reduce the misunderstandings that occur when emotional, factual, and logical input is not identified as being of these distinct types. The following is a distillation of the six hats method:

1. *White hat (neutral and objectivity):* hard data, facts and figures, and questions/suggestions about what data to collect.
2. *Yellow hat (logical positive):* savings, benefits, and advantages. Usually forward thinking.

3. *Green hat (creative):* proposals, suggestions, ideas, alternatives, and provocations, what is interesting in an idea.
4. *Red hat (emotional and initiative):* hunches, feelings, soft data, and emotional things (e.g. discussing something that makes the discussion participant angry, etc).
5. *Black hat (logical negative):* caution, rationale for not doing something, why it may go wrong, legal limits, etc.
6. *Blue hat (meta-hat):* control, organization of the discussion process and use of the other hats. Blue hat use can suggest a particular structure to a discussion ("2 minutes of white hat, then 5 minutes of yellow"). Or off the cuff material. The blue hat can also be used for conclusions.

The objective of using this six hats method is to produce stakeholder problem scenarios that can be used in the formulation of proposals to various stakeholder groups when the need arises. These scenarios can also be used to formulate proposals to the senior management and project teams.

(Information on the six hats method can be obtained from the Executive Administrator, The Edward De Bono Foundation, P.O. Box 2397, Dublin 8.)

3.6.2 Gaining acceptance

To ensure successful implementation of your proposal, it is necessary to gain maximum acceptance. Remember, any proposal has little value until it is put to use. Consider the following, how should you alter or modify your proposal so it will be as acceptable as possible to those it will affect and to those who will pass judgement on it? Ask yourself the following questions along with others that are relevant.

- Whom does the proposal affect?
- What major obstacles will I confront?
- How might I overcome any obstacles?
- What might go wrong?
- Why would something go wrong?
- What can I do to prevent problems?
- What opportunities might present themselves?
- How might I best gain support for my proposal?
- How might I best present and sell my proposal?
- What should I not do?

Develop your plan of action and follow through. Remember, the proactive individual makes the right things happen on time.

Gather the best thoughts from your acceptance finding and develop your sequential plan of action. Establish start dates and target end dates. Decide who will be responsible for each task. Set out your checkpoints to see if events are happening according to plan.

(See Parnes, S.J. (1967) Creative Behaviour Guidebook, New York, Charles Scribner's Sons.)

3.7 Addressing stakeholder information needs

In complex or large software projects where stakeholders are numerous access to information is perhaps the most overriding stakeholder need. Research undertaken by McManus (2004) found that the majority of stakeholders did not receive adequate information from the project manager or delegated staff. It was found that barriers existed between the project team and the stakeholders in both oral and written communications. Extended stakeholder groups reported that written information was too technical and not usable for improving decision-making practices.

My own experience is that face-to-face communication is the most effective and allows stakeholders to air their concerns without resorting to other forms of communication such as e-mails where the contents (at times) can be ambiguous and may lead to mis-understandings and conflict, if not coached in sensitive language. As an example, I recall a project manager working on a govern-ment-related project. This manager needed clarification on a number of technical issues. Some days passed without commu-nication from the project sponsor. In "frustration" the project manager sent the sponsor an e-mail outlining his frustrations with their lack of response. The fallout from this e-mail resulted in the project manager losing out on career progression and future project opportunities. The point here is do not let your emotions take the place of logic and clear thinking. Moments of frustration and/or madness can be costly.

3.7.1 Developing a stakeholder communication strategy

All projects whether large or small benefit from the develop-ment of a communication strategy. Communication is not just a matter of making effective presentations, holding meetings, or handing down information. It is about creating trust and develop-ing a climate in which open communication can take place.

Developing an effective communications stakeholder involvement strategy is an effort that requires assembling a selection of techniques to meet the needs of a given project. When designing your stakeholder communication strategy it is recommended to pursue a systematic thought process based on fundamental guidelines and following a series of steps. The recommended guidelines are:

- *Acting in accord with basic democratic principle:* means that involvement is more than simply following legislation and regulations. In a democratic society, people have opportunities to debate issues, frame alternative solutions, and affect final decisions in ways that respect the roles of decision-maker and knowledge is the basis of such participation, through continued interaction with the entire community.
- *Continuous contact between the stakeholder community:* throughout project decision-making, from the earliest stages, as one or more project problems are identified, through defining purpose and need or planning principles, through the development of a range of potential solutions, and up to the decision to implement a particular solution.
- *Use of a variety of involvement techniques that target different stakeholder groups or individuals*: in different ways or target the same groups or individuals in different ways. A single one-size-fits-all approach usually results in missing many people.
- *Active outreach to stakeholders means we search out the stakeholder and work hard to illicit response:* resources tend to be limited, and managers cannot make anyone participate. However, managers have repeatedly found that going after the stakeholder and changing unsuccessful approaches brings greater results.
- *Focusing participation on decisions rather than on conducting participation activities because they are required:* decisions include both the continuous stream of informal decisions made by the project manager and other management and the less frequent formal decisions made by decision-makers. Timely response to ideas from the stakeholders and integration of ideas from the stakeholders into decisions shows the stakeholders that participation is worthwhile. A focus on the wide range of possible decisions gets the project manager past simply offering the stakeholder passive opportunities to comment on proposals just before formal decision-making.

The following steps form one approach to systematically setting up and implementing a stakeholder involvement strategy for projects.

- *Set goals and objectives for stakeholder involvement:* the goals and objectives derive from the specific circumstances of a given plan, or project. What decisions, formal or informal, are to be made? When? And by whom? What stakeholder input is needed? Stakeholder input can be in the form of a consensus on a plan or a build able project. Consensus does not mean that everyone agrees enthusiastically but that all influential groups and individuals can live with a proposal. Stakeholder input can be in the form of information used by staff or decision-makers. Management use the objectives to form the stakeholder involvement programme. The more specific the objectives, the better they will guide the involvement programme.

- *Identify the people to be reached:* the general stakeholder community and those directly affected, such as primary stakeholders, are some of those who should be reached. Review who is affected directly and indirectly, as well as those who have shown past interest. Look for people who do not traditionally participate, such as minority groups. What information do they need to participate? What issues or decisions affect which specific groups or individuals? How can their ideas be incorporated into decisions? New individuals and groups appear throughout a stakeholder involvement programme; there should be a way to identify and involve them. Conceptualize the stakeholder as a collection of discrete groups, individuals, and the general stakeholder, each has different interests and different levels of energy for participation.

  Usually, these two steps interact and are conducted simultaneously. In addition to brainstorming and analysis by project staff, ask members of the stakeholder community for their input on goals, objectives, and names of people who might be interested. This can be done through key person interviews or focus groups or stakeholder opinion surveys.

- *Develop a general approach or set of general strategies that are keyed to the goals and objectives of the communication strategy and the characteristics of the target audiences:* strategies should fit the target audience in terms of what input is desired and the level of interest. Approaches should take into consideration resources of time, money, and staff. A general approach can be visualized in terms of a principle technique; for example, an Extranet or web site. It could be visualized as a stream of different activities keyed to specific user needs or project decisions. Alternatively, a general approach could be viewed as a focus on one or more stakeholder groups or interests. Project managers should at least check with members of the stakeholder community for ideas on our general approach and whether the stakeholder to be reached finds the approach acceptable.

- *Flesh out the approach with specific techniques:* consult past experience for what works and does not work. Look at best practice communication techniques. Obtain ideas from other project managers that have had successful experiences with stakeholder involvement. The project manager should choose techniques that fit our specific purpose.

- *Assure those proposed communication strategies and techniques aid decision-making to close the loop:* ask project staff the following questions:
  - Are many people participating with good ideas?
  - Are key groups participating?
  - Is the stakeholder getting enough information as a basis for meaningful input?
  - Are decision-makers getting adequate stakeholder information when it is needed?
  - Ask participants who is missing from the participation process. How can missing participants be attracted?
  - Do participants think discussion is full and complete? Do they think the project is responsive?
  - Is participation regarding? If not, why not? Continually evaluate and make mid-course corrections.

3.7.1.1 Some benefits of stakeholder communication strategies

The benefits of a stakeholder communication strategy includes:

- expanding stakeholder understanding of the project
- gaining greater insight into the project
- helping to clarify things
- refocusing attention on the project
- helping stakeholders put together pieces of information they have heard
- helping stakeholders better understand why do something
- reinforcing experience
- challenging stakeholders to rethink
- helping stakeholders develop an answer to a problem
- providing interest in learning more about the project
- stimulating stakeholders to think about the topic/problem in a new way
- providing ammunition to use in an argument
- triggering ideas based on the information
- providing confidence in what stakeholders already know

- helping stakeholders apply what they know to a new situation
- encouraging stakeholders to act on what they know
- providing confidence to tell someone else what they believe
- helping stakeholders understand project managers better.

3.8 Chapter summary – 10 key points

The most important points to take away from this chapter are as follows. Remember:

1. capability in project management is about providing products and services that are fit for purpose
2. competency is created when resources are deployed into those activities associated with the delivery of those products and services
3. core competences should not be seen as fixed
4. optimization should be about improving individual competencies and finding innovative ways inform and motivate people and their capabilities
5. commitment on the part of stakeholders is a necessary determinant for successes in software projects
6. stakeholder interests should be connected to the appropriate project stage or phase
7. one aspect of power is about getting things done, power should be used to gain favour with stakeholders and to form partnerships or alliances
8. the challenge when faced with stakeholder problems is to move from a generalized approach to focused situation that can be acted upon
9. proposals to stakeholders are of little value if they cannot be acted upon
10. develop a stakeholder strategy (and plan) and follow through, and to set goals and objectives for stakeholder involvement.

Chapter reading

Baker, B., D. Murphy, and D. Fisher (1983) Factors Affecting Project Success.

Clegg, S.R. (1997) Frameworks of Power, Sage Publications, UK.

Cleland, D. and W. King (eds), Project Management Handbook, Van Nostrand Reinhold.

Ferry, D.J. and P.S. Brandon (1991) Cost Planning of Buildings (6th edition). Oxford, Blackwell Scientific Publications.

French, J.R.P. and B. Raven (1959) The bases of social power. In Studies of Social Power. Cartwright, D (ed.), Ann Arbor, MI, The University of Michigan, pp. 150–167.

Grady, R. (1997) Successful Software Process Improvement, Prentice Hall Publication.

Kipnis, D. (1976). The Power Holders. Chicago, IL, University of Chicago Press.

Moss Kanter, R. (1985) The Change Masters: Innovation and entrepreneurship in the American Corporation. New York, Simon Schuster.

Newman, M. and R. Sabherwal (1996) Determinants of commitment to information systems development: a longitudinal investigation. MIS Quarterly, 20, 23–54.

O'Reilly, C. and J. Chatman (1986) Organizational commitment and psychological attachment: the effects of compliance, identification, and internalization on pro-social behaviour. Journal of Applied Psychology, 7, 492–499.

Willer, D., M.J. Lovaglia, and B. Markovsky (1997) Power and influence: a theoretical bridge. Social Forces, 76, 571–603.

4   Instruments of Stakeholder Analysis

4.1 Review on stakeholder analysis

Before moving on to Section 4.2, I would briefly like to revisit some key points of stakeholder analysis. In Chapter 2 we reviewed the key components of what constituted a basic stakeholder analysis. To recap the first step in a stakeholder analysis is to *identify* (Section 2.1) and list all potential stakeholders (internal, external, and extended). The second step (Section 2.2) focused on how we attract and *classify* stakeholders using maps and checklists and other qualitative information and analysis techniques. The third step focused on how we achieve stakeholder *participation and involvement* (Section 2.3). In Section 3.3 we discussed some of the barriers to stakeholder commitment.

In this chapter we will focus on the fourth step of *maintain* that is the question of how to satisfy stakeholders and their ongoing needs? In answering this question the discussion will open those topics of stakeholder values and behaviours, ethics, legitimacy, and project governance.

4.2 Stakeholder values and behaviours

As stated in Section 1.2.2 (Figure 1.5), project managers should support processes and modes of behaviour that are sympathetic, sensitive, and respectful to stakeholders and their needs.

Values and behaviours are often associated with what behaviourists call "higher needs" that is trust, motivation, empowerment, success, relationships, and influence. People (including external and extended stakeholders) are a project organization's only real resource. It is the individuals associated with any project who create and implement ideas. Without them, nothing would exist: there would be no memory, no strength, and no advantage. The basic value, which is so important, is *respect for people*.

As pointed out individuals have rights and duties, and the most essential of these is the right to do an excellent job coupled with the duty to do so with satisfaction.

Guilmette *et al.* (1996) and McManus (2002) identify eight stakeholder values, these are as follows:

1. Power rests with ideas. Ideas, much more than financial resource, should dominate agenda, and policy should stem from a great vision.
2. Respect for knowledge and intellectual rigour. Ideas do not come freely: they mature in the painstaking search for facts, concrete experience, and respect for know-how.
3. Relevance remains the most fundamental value. When all richness, beauty, and power are lost only relevance remains to justify human intelligence.
4. Anticipation preserves relevance. The tendency to make decisions based on outdated information leads inevitably to an "irrelevant" response to perpetual evolution. Forward thinking is vital if we wish to focus on action, anticipate danger and opportunities, and especially allow the project organization to take its destiny into its own hands.
5. The search for excellence develops the necessary leadership. Many decisions cannot be made except in a climate of uncertainty. This uncertainty constitutes a serious handicap when people must be convinced of the usefulness of taking complex avenues and risks that cannot really be evaluated except intuitively, based on past experience. The sustained pursuit of excellence, and the recruitment and training of top-notch employees, is essential to building up such leadership.
6. Integrity is preserved by the search for productivity. Integrity is a moral virtue that is paramount to any successful project undertaking. Without integrity, there is nothing but lies and sloth. The true search for productivity constitutes a subtle tool for preserving integrity.
7. To be efficient, attention must be directed towards goals. Action must be strategic, precise, and properly focused.
8. Nothing can better preserve these values than the relentless pursuit of the mission.

Values provide a form of guidance system in that values are actually part of an individual's personality, especially if some values dominate over others. Values are inherited and/or acquired from parents, peer groups, media, and other environmental surroundings as well as from our own experiences and observations.

Values determine how we make judgements. Values can be categorized as political, economic, social, technical, cultural, religious, etc. Most project managers and other individuals form a hierarchy of values of which some are more dominant in our decision-making than others. For example, those project managers with economic values may view the use of a group of stakeholders for a particular set of activities as an efficient use of resources, while other project managers with social values upper most may consider the same group as an asset because of their level of knowledge, skills, flexibility, and social cohesion (Jayaratna, 1996, p. 25).

Organizations in which project managers (or other stakeholders) are expected to solve problems may demonstrate implicit or explicit value systems. Usually, these values are set by key decision-makers through policies they devise and through explicit behaviour they demand or encourage within a project. Figure 4.1 provides a view of the interrelationship between values and behaviours.

In any projects day-to-day activities stakeholder values are "passive participants" in that the individual stakeholder is not generally aware of the role their values are playing in the project life cycle. When decisions are made it is argued that values play a passive role except when the project manager or decision-maker is called upon to make strategic decisions where value judgements are called for. For example, the allocation of scarce resources is such a decision, particularly when there are competing demands. A crucial question that project managers have to ask is "to what extent do the individually held values of their stakeholders predetermine the decisions?"

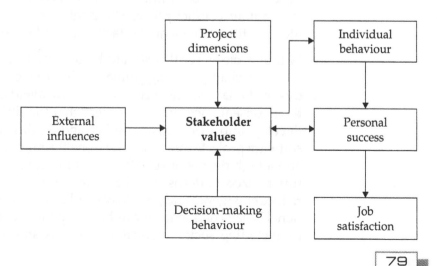

Figure 4.1
Relationships between values and behaviours.

If strategic project choices have a large behavioural component, then to some extent they reflect the idiosyncrasies of decision-makers. Hambrick and Mason (1984), maintain that values are part of the decision-makers cognitive base, values are part of the essence of the person, they act on their daily lives. The project manager only really becomes aware of them when stakeholders challenge them, such as when a strategic choice that involves a conflict of their values has to be made. Many project managers, even at this point, may not be aware as to why they are experiencing inner turmoil over the decision.

4.3 Conflict and loyalties

Behaviours and values can be both an integrating and conflict creating force. In most instances, interactions between the project manager and project stakeholders may help to change individual's dominant values; hence the chance of a compromise and a consensus between parties is achievable. However, when a number of stakeholders with conflicting values refuse to change their value priorities and continue to judge the same situation from their strongly held individual value perspectives, then they create for themselves "ill structured situations and conflict".

Among the variety of definitions of conflict offered, two definitions are found particularly fruitful when addressing conflict between the project and its stakeholders. One is applied by Thamhain and Wilemon (1975) where conflict is defined as *the process, which begins when one party perceives that the other has frustrated, or is about to frustrate, some concern of his.* Our other definition is suggested by Deutsch (1973); *a conflict exists whenever incompatible activities occur.* Together these definitions address both the behavioural or attitudinal side and the inappropriateness of stakeholder conflict *per se.* These initial statements about conflict constitute an adequate starting point for further discussion.

Within projects conflict should be regarded as a virus in stakeholder exchange having primarily disruptive, dissociating and dysfunctional consequences. The aim is to avoid conflict or reduce their consequences because of fear that too little coherence can develop into destructive conflict and a diffusion of focus. In software projects this is usually done through detailed contracts and a high degree of specification. Price mechanisms and institutionalized patterns of behaviour are used as instruments to reduce emergence and growth of conflict. In recent years new relational based contractual forms have supplied formal mechanisms by including social interaction elements and relational norms.

The main point is, however, that conflict should be avoided but how?

The project manager must identify those stakeholders that pose a potential threat (future conflict situation) to the project. Any actions taken by the project manager to counter stakeholder threats must be properly concentrated and focused. So how do stakeholders present potential threats to the project and project manager? They do so by:

- not treating the project manager with respect
- not informing the project manager of their concerns
- not providing adequate data or adequate information
- using poor management practices
- making statements before informing the project manager
- failing to be open and honest with the project manager
- not providing alternatives in an objective manner
- not adjusting to the new reality of an involved situation
- not supporting the project manager – lack of loyalty
- springing surprises at meetings
- having hidden agendas.

4.3.1 Conflict resolution

From a sociological point of view conflict is a social phenomena, and neither the occurrence nor the outcome of the conflict is completely and rigidly determined by the objective circumstances. On the other hand the importance of "real conflict" cannot be denied. Nevertheless, the psychological process of perceiving and evaluating are also real, and they are involved in turning objective conditions into experienced conflict. Two processes can be related to the phenomenon of conflict (Deutsch, 1973).

The first process deals with the coupling between the real situation and the conflict as such. This process, caused by the situation, can develop into either a conflict or a direct solution. In many instances a situation leading to a solution is favourable. On the other hand some argue that the process should sometimes be allowed to develop into a conflict prior to solution thus opening up new ideas and alternatives. The crucial question is what kind of forces drives the process into a constructive pattern, and what does not? The second process deals with the coupling between the conflict and solution. For example, when dealing with your stakeholders, or even your project team, it is important to always keep in mind the idea that both parties are (or should be) seeking a win/win situation. No one wants to feel like they are giving away something for nothing. In fact, most conflicts arise because one party feels like the other party is taking advantage of them. In order to avoid these types of situations, there are certain principles you can apply to increase your chances of a successful resolution:

- *Avoid defend–attack interaction:* these tend to be non-productive every time
- *Seek more information:* ask a lot of questions
- *Check your understanding and summarize:* make sure that you are understanding everything
- *Try to understand the stakeholder's perspective:* communication is more than just listening; try to see it their way

In essence:

- Try to determine if there is a problem between you and the stakeholder.
- If you think there is a problem, set up a private face-to-face meeting to discuss the problem with the stakeholder.
- In a no confrontational manner, ask the stakeholder if there is a problem. If his/her answer is "no", inform the stakeholder that you think there is a problem and explain what you think the problem is.
- As you talk, ask for feedback. Do not "attack" the stakeholder with accusations.
- Try to listen to each other with open minds.
- Be sure to respect each other's opinions.
- Take a few minutes to recycle the stakeholder's opinions in your mind.
- Try to determine why the stakeholder felt the way they did.
- Avoid "finger-pointing".
- Try to work out a compromise that pleases both of you.

4.3.2 Loyalty

In Section 3.5 it was stated that: *power is relative in the sense that the source of the project manager's power lies not in himself, but in his followers."* If the project manager is to gain favour and deliver a success outcome he must encourage and secure loyalty from all people working on the project. Take the following advice given by Machiavelli in 1512:

> But confining myself more to the particular, I say that a prince may be seen happy to-day and ruined to-morrow without having shown any

change of disposition or character. This, I believe, arises firstly from causes that have already been discussed at length, namely, that the prince who relies entirely on fortune is lost when it changes. I believe also that he will be successful who directs his actions according to the spirit of the times, and that he whose actions do not accord with the times will not be successful. Because men are seen, in affairs that lead to the end which every man has before him, namely, glory and riches, to get thereby various methods; one with caution, another with haste; one by force, another by skill; one by patience, another by its opposite; and each one succeeds in reaching the goal by a different method. One can also see of two cautious men the one attain his end, the other fail; and similarly, two men by different observances are equally successful, the one being cautious, the other impetuous; all this arises from nothing else than whether or not they conform in their methods to the spirit of the times. This follows from what I have said, that two men working differently bring about the same effect, and of two working similarly, one attains his object and the other does not.
(Nicolo Machiavelli's the PRINCE (1512), Chapter XXV, Translated by Marriott, W.K. 1998.)

Although written 500 years ago Machiavelli's advice holds true today. In that without loyalty the project manager in the long term is likely "not to succeed". Building lasting and loyal relationships with stakeholders is intrinsic to securing the long-term security of a project. Historically, the emphasis within commercial organizations has been narrower, with maximization of financial and shareholder value being seen as the key priority for most private sector companies. However, changing social pressures mean that project managers can no longer focus solely on their budgets and performance as the key benchmark for continued successful existence.

In securing loyalty the project manager is advised to distinguish between different types of stakeholder relationships, stretching from the positive to the negative side of these relationships, but how? One way to create and test loyalty is through the use of empowerment. Empowering people gives them a sense of respect, purpose and definition, which places them in positions power and influence this strategy is more likely to secures their loyalty in the long term and will allow the project manager to measure their contribution more objectively and directly.

A less direct and confrontational method of measuring stakeholder loyalty is by relating the various relational factors in the form of a grid (Figure 4.2); that is, behaviour orientation, attitudes, trust, communication, learning, power, reciprocity, and commitment, which shape a specific relationship. Alternatively maintain a chronology (or diary) of key relationships and how those

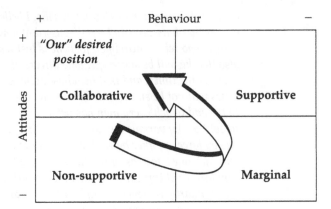

Figure 4.2 Example of a loyalty grid.

relationships were handled noting any events that were difficult and how such events were resolved – learning from the experiences recorded.

4.4 Ethics in stakeholder relationships

Every philosophy (including project management) is measured not only by what it achieves, but also by its aspirations. For instance, the attainment of complete or perfect truth as positioned by analysis and agreement is by itself an ideal. The fundamental measures of performance of both analysis and agreement, which they take as objectives, are instead ideals. Ideals represent the highest aims and aspirations of humankind. They function not only as intellectual, moral, aesthetic guideposts, but more deeply, as spiritual aides (Mitroff and Linstone, 1993, p. 154).

Mitroff together with Mason has been a pioneer in the use of stakeholder concept – especially in strategic management. Mason *et al.* (1995) argues that all ethical questions arise initially out of human agency. Technology, due to its capability to augment mental and physical powers of human beings, does stand in the role of a co-conspirator. The lure of power-enhancing capabilities makes technology an inducer of sorts, a necessary but not sufficient underpinning to many of the ethical issues we face today. An ethical issue is said to arise *whenever one party in pursuit of its goals engages in behaviour that materially affects the ability of another party to pursue its goals.* When the effect is helpful – good, right, just – we say the behaviours are praiseworthy or exemplary. When, however, the effect is harmful – bad, wrong, unjust – the behaviour is unethical. This purposeful theory of ethics is reflected in the issues discussed in previous sections.

For example, e-mail and being online are applications of information technology, the lure of which is based on their ability to expand the scope, range, speed, and ease of interpersonal and corporate communications.

One case where ethical concerns have been explicitly related to the stakeholder concept is in the work undertaken by Rackley *et al.* They review the conflicts of loyalty that a computer professional may face when clients, users, and stakeholders are affected differently by a system and suggest that the fundamental obligation of professionals is to minimize harm to others. This is particularly important in software engineering because of the great impact many contemporary computer systems have on people.

4.4.1 Ethical thoughts

Some academics and practitioners subscribe to the view that being an ethical person and making sound ethical decisions is enough; furthermore, they believe good project managers are by definition ethical leaders. However, this is not necessarily true. For example, Fulton (1998) states:

> *The dilemma we all face every day, having to choose between action that benefits our own self-interest, and action that addresses our obligation to one another: our self-interest, including the need to profit from our dealings with others, versus the "moral" perspective, the social contract that binds us to others.*

The project manager as a moral person is characterized in terms of individual traits; as a moral manager, he is thought of as conveying an ethics message that stakeholders take notice of in their views and behaviours. The basis of ethical leadership is being an ethical person. Stakeholders must think of you as having certain traits, engaging in certain kinds of behaviours, and making decisions based upon ethical principles. Moreover, this ethical self must be authentic. Ethical traits relating to trust include: moral order, integrity, honesty, fairness, and fulfilment of obligations.

While traits are clearly important, behaviours are equally important. Behaviours include: doing the right thing, showing concern for people and treating people right being open and communicative, and demonstrating morality in one's personal life. In the decision-making role, project managers should have a set of ethical values and principles; they should aim to be unbiased and reasonable. A project manager's decisions should look beyond the balance sheet; the "moral person" represents the essence of the ethical manager.

Project managers need to recognize the importance of pro-actively putting ethics at the forefront of their stakeholder agenda; project managers need to make the ethical dimension of their leadership explicit and salient to their subordinates. The ethical project manager can be achieved by serving as a visible and vocal role model for ethical conduct and ethical management can be achieved using a reward system holding all employees accountable to ethical standards.

The ethical project manager must be both a moral person and a moral manager. This manager is both a substantively ethical person and a leader who makes ethics and values a prominent part of the leadership agenda. Ethical management is good for the project and avoids problem, for example legal, later, and contributes to team commitment and satisfaction. The project manager must also find ways to focus the stakeholders' attention on ethics and values and to instil the project management team with the principles to guide their actions.

4.5 Central ethical issues

In today's regulated climate an ethical project manager is essential now more than ever (see also Section 4.5.4). The major criticism of current project practice is that any ethical consideration tends to be implicit rather than explicit which has a tendency to devalue the importance of the ethical dimension. In his book, *Ethics of Information Management* (p. 98), Mason identifies four ethical issues which are pertinent to the project manager they are:

1. temptation
2. ethical quandaries
3. criticism
4. professional self-regulation.

4.5.1 Temptation

Project managers are often faced with moments of truth; such moments of truth may be associated with moral decisions such as telling a client (or not) that the project is at risk, or that the project is predicted to be 6 months late. We all face moments of truth in our day-to-day lives how we deal with these moments of truth is our moral responsibility. One of the roles of ethical thinking is to help us recognize temptations and thereby avoid them. Some ethicists believe that leaders of organizations have a moral obligation to safeguard their members from common temptations. Such might include the temptation:

- to deceive
- to cheat
- not to keep your promises
- to work outside the law
- not to do your duty.

The ethical issues surrounding temptations are more profound than they often appear at the outset, but they are comparatively easy to resolve, they simply involve distinguishing right from wrong but for many of us this is easier said than done, and sometimes this requires the wisdom of Solomon.

4.5.2 Ethical quandaries

Ethical quandaries sometimes referred to as dilemma usually force the project manager or stakeholders to make choices between undesirable alternatives. The distinction between quandary and dilemma is not merely semantic. According to Mason quandaries are a richer and more perplexing state in which there may be many different directions to turn, each of which is laced with bad and good implications.

A typical ethical quandary faced by managers and stakeholders alike is that associated with a conflict of interest. For example consider the following case involving one consultancy in the US.

A corporation with which the firm had been consulting on a number of human resource management systems issues over a couple of years, informed them that they were merging with two other national firms. They requested a proposal for providing them a performance valuation system that would integrate the systems of the three corporations and could be used for a gain-sharing programme. Their proposal reflected an empirically supported methodology and intervention(s) that had been successfully utilized with our client 2 years earlier. Within a week of submission of the proposal they met with them to learn that while they appreciated the scientific rigour and deliverables, they wanted them to compress the project to 3 weeks and reduce the performance evaluation system to a one-page evaluation format that would assess all members on the same dimensions regardless of the qualifications, position, and the job responsibilities. To meet the new deadlines and deliverables they offered a six-figure bonus to the contract. The company declined on multiple bases and they contracted with another firm. The firm concerned would not compromise on the required methodology, and would not collapse multiple performance dimensions to an unsubstantiated system, and a system that would be plagued with future problems although it might appear expedient at the time.

(Source: The consulting psychologist, 5(1), Spring 2003.)

4.5.3 Criticism

Project managers face reactive situations, ones in which they must take the initiative. Those more mature software organizations will have policies and procedures that tend to promote "unethical" behaviour. For example, project managers (and members of their team) tend to have access to large amounts of confidential information, which they could use to their advantage or to damage individuals. To counter such situations organizations enforce policies that protect personnel data such as the Data Protection Act. Where breaches in policy do occur criticism usually follows in the form of reports in which individual managers and other employees usually face sanctions or dismissal.

4.5.4 Professional self-regulation

Some project managers and other software professionals will hold membership of professional bodies such as the Project Management Institute, Association of Project Managers and British Computer Society. Professional bodies such as these have an interest in upholding and promoting ethical and professional practices. For example, in October 2002, the British Computer Society (BCS) Chief Executive David Clarke said the major BCS drive in the "next 5 years" would be in promoting information systems as a profession. He said:

> *There is no reason why IS should not be seen in the same light as health and law, he said. We have not tried to become that profession in the past, we have not set the standards and ethics that other professions have. Professionalism means delivering what we said we would, on time and to budget. It means having the right skills available, commitment to continuing professional development, following a code of practice, and recognised qualifications.*

More recently the BCS has established a specialist interest group to look at ethical behaviour in the use of information systems. A recent survey undertaken by De Montfort University (2003), in the UK generated speculation that young IT professionals have less concern about ethics as they struggle to get their careers established – if true, this represents a significant challenge for all peer managers.

4.5.4.1 Ethical attributes

Professional and large software organizations will generally have codes of conduct that cover ethical behaviour that includes guidance on how to conduct oneself professionally. Ethical attributes associated with codes of conduct include:

1. contributions to society and humankind
2. avoid causing harm to others
3. avoid discrimination
4. respect intellectual property rights
5. respect the privacy of others
6. respect agreements
7. respect the confidentiality of others
8. maintain professional standards
9. maintain professional competence
10. maintain confidentiality of information.

If a specific course of action committed by a manager or stakeholder fails to fulfil any of those ethical attributes above then the action can be defined as unethical. English law unfortunately does little to inhibit those managers that break the rules or outrage society and few company managers or corporate stakeholders end up in the courts charged with professional misconduct. Policing and disciplining professionals is by large left with the professional institutions to administer. The down side here is that few individuals relish the unpleasant task of disciplining fellow members.

In their day-to-day activities project managers should impose a degree of self-regulation in what they do and how they act and behave to others. They should also protect themselves against harmful acts of discrimination and take positive steps to update themselves on legislative acts that involve breaches in criminal, moral, or human rights.

4.6 Legitimacy and project governance

The term "governance" refers to the processes and structure used to direct and manage an organizations operations and activities. It defines the division of power, and establishes the mechanisms to achieve accountability between stakeholders, the board of directors and management. Good governance systems help organizations focus on the activities which contribute most to their overall objectives: to utilize their resources effectively and ensure they are managed in the best interests of their principal stakeholders. At corporate level good governance is about:

- respect for human rights and the rule of law
- strengthening democracy
- promoting transparency and capacity in private and public administration.

For those of "us" you work in software engineering or emerging technologies (such as e-commerce, etc.) governance presents unprecedented challenges in political, economic, and societal systems. Two key UK reports one by Cadbury the other by Turnbull highlighted a number of issues and recommended a number of changes. They included:

1. Cadbury (1992)
   - Separate audit and remuneration committees
   - Audit committee meet with auditors
   - Disclosure remuneration of directors accounts
   - Three year term of office
   - Non-executives have funds to take external advice
2. Turnbull (1999)
   - Accountability for disasters and crises
   - Risk to company must be disclosed
   - Directors must have effective system of internal controls
   - Consultation with board members
   - Provide the senior management and board with early warning mechanisms; and monitor the system of internal control.

It is clear that the software engineering industry is not always benevolent, and regulation can be an effective way to serve societal objectives. But regulating the software industry can be challenging and can have unintended consequences, which may be troublesome to society as the problem of regulations, were intended to prevent.

The underlying implication in the corporate governance proposition is that we share enough common values that society can agree on good governance. In practice, however, only dramatic failures provide the basis for change, and this basis is known to be poor. For example, global scandals make headlines daily. Many of the recent incidents have one thing in common: they are a matter of ethics – or a lack thereof. To combat this, many global business are creating codes of conduct, like the ones such companies as IBM, Xerox and Shell Oil have had for years. These three companies, and others, including Levi Strauss, Honeywell, Digital Equipment, Siemens, Nortel, ITT Corporation, Matsushita Electric, and Canon are taking their efforts further – by incorporating their messages into everyday business practices and making them living documents with global applicability.

Accommodating the principles outlined raises difficulties (that is challenges) and opportunities for those who would offer governance issues in project management. So what is project governance and how can it be used to ensure the successful delivery of software projects?

4.6.1 Project governance

Within software engineering and project management governance covers a number functional disciplines that include:

- corporate strategy
- operations (all services and products)
- resource management
- stakeholder relationships
- professional standards
- security and information
- project boards.

Taking into consideration the number of failed software projects that have been reported in the computer press in the last 5 years. The focus within project management is increasingly moving towards developments in "good practice" which are orienting to an inclusive approach in itself a form of governance based on engagement with stakeholders. Specifically the project management organizations should develop and manage its system of governance so that it facilitates:

- stakeholders with a legitimate interest in the organizations activities and projects
- stakeholders opinions must be valued and taken into account without compromising the organizations ability to make effective and just decisions
- stakeholder engagement in helping to define and shape improvements in delivery and performance
- stakeholder empowerment in delivering positive outcomes.

Project governance objectives should be incorporated into the formal "terms of reference" of the project manager. They should also form part of the project initiation document or PID. Including specific, measurable, achievable, relevant, and time related (SMART) objectives into the appraisal system allows the organization to measure the governance benefits for those products or services you are contracted to provide.

So what benefits can be expected from incorporating project governance into your systems of operation. Project governance helps:

- reduce project risk
- stimulates higher levels of stakeholder involvement
- improves access to markets
- enhances local performance
- improves leadership
- demonstrates transparency and accountability.

Within project governance, risk, transparency, and accountability lie not only with the sponsoring organization but also with "project boards" and such project boards are initiated to manage risk. Some boards by the nature of the mission of the organization require a certain number of people to come from a certain group or profession. Some project-related organizations will require a certain number of key business users on the board. For example, in large rail transportation projects membership of the board is likely to be made up from:

- transport for London
- network rail
- strategic rail authority
- train operating companies
- rail forums.

When this is the case, it is advisable to select candidates carefully with their risk quotient in mind. It is fine to have cautious or risk-taking people on the board, but it is equally important to have a balance. Only in this way can the board incorporate governance and produce balanced decisions time after time. Almost all strategic project decisions involve risk analysis, even if that analysis is taken for granted and dealt with/without ever mentioning risk analysis.

A suggested integrated model for project governance is set out in Figure 4.3.

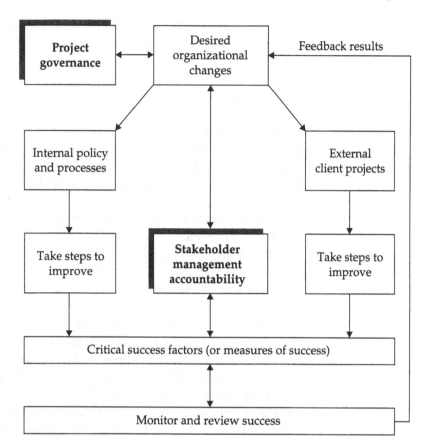

Figure 4.3
Model of integrated perspectives on project governance.

4.7 Managing stakeholder adjustments

The model defined in Figure 4.3 suggests that project governance places considerable accountability on stakeholders to make adjustments to their way of conducting business and doing things in synchronization with the providing organization. In making any such adjustments stakeholders and their organizations will need to consider trade-offs in at least four areas:

1. Business (e.g. strategy and policy)
2. Financial (e.g. trading partners and markets)
3. Operations (e.g. business continuity and liability)
4. Compliance (e.g. business regulations and litigation).

Making adjustments to business practices and other processes must fit the circumstances of the organization. Project stakeholders may therefore decide that only some of the suggested practices are appropriate to their circumstances. This is not to suggest that the practices described in Section 4.6 should be adopted in their totality. It is simply a question of trade-off.

It should be noted that such trade-offs would be influenced by a number of factors, these factors are likely to be risk related and will include:

- an awareness of the organization's objectives and related significant risks
- the organization's policy on risk
- whether the project and management strategies are effective and what needs to be done to put them into effect
- the fundamentals of good process and project management practices
- the scope of management and internal financial control
- the ways in which improvements can be made in order to mitigate the significant risks affecting the ability of the company to achieve its business objectives
- propensity to change behaviours and working practices.

Two ways consultation can help identify whether senior management has identified all the significant trade-offs and risks relevant to the objectives, particularly having regard to the changing internal and external environment. It also provides the "project board" with a sound foundation for its review of the effectiveness of internal control and for its "reporting and communication" to non-board members on control.

4.8 The role of communication

Following on from our discussion in Section 3.7.1, communication is enriched or restricted by the atmosphere between people. An effective project manager will strive to create a sense of openness, encouraging individuals to listen attentively to others or to speak out, knowing their opinions are valued. Effective communication builds on such a culture enabling good debate, bringing out the best in ideas and creativity, and creating the ingredients for the most effective decision-making.

In any project there is a great deal of information that has to be absorbed through the written word. For example, reports, memos, e-mails, technical specifications, plans, etc. To be effective, a project manager needs to read such information with understanding in order to take action or to recall it appropriately and disseminate it concisely and accurately.

As previously stated in Section 3.7, information is also a source of economical and political power within projects and the ability of a project manager to communicate effectively is important because it is the means by which information is transferred between parties.

Communication models the underlying values that a manager holds towards those who look to her/him for authority. The values that form the basis of the project manager's communication will determine whether those who receive their authority from them will receive the information they need when they need it. Thus, the expression of those values will determine whether the project team is successful, fulfilled, both or neither.

The core values of the communication model should be affirmation, involvement, and servant leadership. When these values drive the project manager's communication process, the information is generous, accurate, and matched to the team's own expression of need for information. The communication process driven by this value system is characterized by a team that is affirmed in their need to know, involved in determining what information is communicated, and supported in their desire to put information to work.

However, when communication is driven by an authoritarian value system where the project manager is expressing values of power, control, manipulation and/or abuse, then we observe a communication process that may deliberately withhold information or communicate information in a manner that requires the team to come back for permission before being able to act. Conversely, having information withheld, receiving partial or inaccurate information and being forced to return to the source of authority for more approval are symptoms of the authoritarian value system. The authoritarian value system is characterized by the source of authority having or taking more power than is needed to succeed with his/her responsibility. This deliberate metering out of information will inevitably lead to less success for the project and fulfilment for the team. Effective project management bows to someone's need for excessive power.

On the other side of the values continuum is the *laissez-faire* value system. Communication driven by this value system will also be inadequate, but the motivation is different. A "laissez-faire" value system tends to abrogate the authority to resource the team with information. The motivation is not control but a tendency to shy away from giving the impression of being in control. The project manager mistakes distance from the team as empowerment of the team. Information is not properly understood to be the vital resource that it is. The team or other stakeholders are left on their own to obtain what information they can.

The distance created by this lack of affirmation, involvement, and support is just as disempowering and de-motivating. Team is disempowered and devalued with the result that success and personal fulfilment are compromized. What is termed as effective project management yields to incompetence?

The concept of "might is right" and "live and let live" values systems are equally dysfunctional. In other words, abusive power and incompetence in the process of communication have the same effect – the loss of effective project management.

In order to manage effectively, a project manager does well to recognize the symptoms of an authoritarian or a laissez-faire value system in his/her own communication process: incomplete, sparse, inaccurate, controlled, manipulated, or false information.

In our understanding of healthy working relationships, the manager is accountable to the team for providing the vital resource of information. That means that the recipient of authority can assist the manager by holding she/he accountable for using a communication process that provides the resource of information that does produce success and personal fulfilment.

As we have said earlier, the value system that drives the communication process is as important as the process itself. Developing an awareness of one's own value system, monitoring the active expression of affirmation, involvement, and servant leadership, will ensure that the communication process will have the desired result of effective project management: success for the organization and a deep sense of satisfaction for the team and the project stakeholders (Stahike, 2001).

4.9 Chapter summary – 10 key points

The most important points to take away from this chapter are as follows. Remember:

1. to be efficient, attention must be directed towards goals. Action must be strategic, precise, and properly focused.
2. that when decisions are being made stakeholder's values play a passive role except when the project manager or decision-maker is called upon to make strategic decisions where value judgements are called for.
3. that it is the project manager's responsibility to identify those stakeholders that pose a potential threat to the project and develop a mitigating course of action.
4. when dealing with your stakeholders, or even your project team, it is important to always keep in mind the idea

that both parties are seeking a win/win to conflict situations.

5. that every philosophy (including project management) is measured not only by what it achieves, but also by its aspirations.
6. that "we" all face moments of truth in our day-to-day lives how we deal with these moments of truth is our moral responsibility.
7. project managers should impose self-regulation in what they do and how they act and behave to others.
8. stakeholder's opinions must be valued and taken into account without compromising the organizations ability to make effective and just decisions.
9. to incorporate project governance objectives into the formal "terms of reference" of the project manager.
10. the values that form the basis of the projects manager's communication will determine whether those who receive their authority from them will receive the information they need when they need it.

Chapter reading

Deutsch, M. (1973) The Resolution of Conflict. New Haven, Yale University Press.

Fulton, J. (1998) Ethics and the 21st Century Manager, Masters Forum.

Guilmette, J.H. *et al.* (1996) Au-delà de l'aide d'urgence: alerte précoce, prévention des conflits et prise de décision, In Actes de La Rencontre Internationale Francophone, Ottawa, 19–22 September 1995. Ottawa, Government of Canada.

Hambrick, D.C. and P.A. Mason (1984) Upper Echelons: The Organisation As a Reflection of Its Top Managers. Academy of Management Review, 9(2), 193–206.

Jayaratna, N. (1996) Choice of Methodology for Information Systems, BCS, IMS UK Conference, pp. 23–28.

Mason, R., F. Mason, and M. Culnan (1995) Ethics of Information Management. Thousand Oaks, California, USA, Sage.

McManus, J. (2002) The Influence of Stakeholder Values on Project Management, Management Services Journal, 8–15.

Mitroff, I. and H. Linstone (1993) The Unbounded Mind, Oxford, England, Oxford University Press.

Stahike, L. (2001) Managing Change Part 2, Governance Matters. com.

Thamhain, H.J. and D.L. Wilemon (1975) Conflict Management in Project Life Cycles, Sloan Management Review Summer.

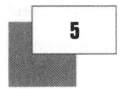

5 Building and Assessing Collaborative Stakeholder Relationships

5.1 Collaborative stakeholder relationships

Some aspects of collaborative relationships have already been covered in Section 2.3.1, I would like to expand on the case already made by discussing some strategic and stakeholder issues of collaborations and alliances.

Positive relationships flourish when the stakeholder management process is undertaken to further the goals and objectives of the organization. It is the process of collaboration and consensus building that is important here. The key is to use the knowledge capital of stakeholders in a productive way and make it inclusive.

Collaborative relationships to some extent have a basis in utilitarianism in that we seek the greatest good for the greatest number. Utilitarianism favours no particular domain, but seeks solutions and strategies that generally benefit all. Its wisdom derives not from revealed truth or accepted rules of engagement, but from a rational dispassionate assessment. It has a Machiavellian flavour because its actions arise from analysis of costs vs. benefits, not those intrinsic values as previously described. In project management utilitarianism makes sense and is good consensus politics (as my good friends Stuart Smith, John Starkie and Neville Jennings, and many others would attest too). Its spirit is often one of compromise that is finding ways to encourage partners and other stakeholders without threatening them; focusing simultaneously on the short-term needs and long-term goals; a belief that commercial forces, because they reflect the will of everyone, will ultimately resolve issues to most people's satisfaction.

The software industry especially those organizations engaged in managed services have seen changes in priorities and strategy towards collaborative relationships this is clearly evident in how senior managers rate the importance of various knowledge workers today versus 5 years ago. In the mid to late 1990s managers across the IT industry placed looking out for number one first and generally favoured going it alone. Today we see more positive collaborations within the industry and shared risk reward (a point we will come back to later) is becoming a popular business model with many software service providers. Why? The most appropriate answer is that collaborations ensure key personnel and other stakeholders are involved in the different stages of the project value-creation chain. To emphasis this point among "my own peer group" there is recognition that global competition is a reality in which satisfying the customer (or client) with quality goods or services is a prerequisite for our long-term survival. For example, the majority of us have witnessed to some degree the vulnerability of organizations to takeovers of various kinds – with the resulting threat to individual jobs and careers. Given the complexity and stress involved in managing software projects, project managers need to look towards more co-operative and collaborative support from peers and external stakeholders alike.

5.1.1 Reflections

Organizations (and those employed within them) are sensitive to changing political, economic, and social and cultural trends. Drucker (1988) observed, that an organization's culture is a function of shared values (and trust, and that trust must be a shared value). Values make a difference in collaborative ventures, because they make a difference about how people feel about themselves and about their work, organization, and country. Values affect our view of the future and about other people, and ultimately our willingness to commit to our responsibilities. If we subscribe to the view that successful stakeholder collaborations are based on trust and trust is based on good relationships that include: addressing conflictual issues, integrating diverse view points, creating mutual benefits, and developing shared power and responsibilities we have a value system and model that starts to create a collaborative environment. Figure 5.1 outlines a simple collaborative model.

5.1.2 Building collaborative relationships

Senge (1990) argued that successful organizations have a vision for what they want to accomplish, a strategy to realize this vision, and the resources needed to support the vision. In building

Model attributes	Type 1: Approach non-inclusive	Type 2: Approach inclusive
Business goals	Project manager takes sole responsibility	Project manager creates responsibility for goals and results
Information	Project manager controls data and information	Project manager is responsive and shares data and information
Resources	Project manager controls (and limits) access to resources	Project manager shares resources with other project managers and links customer and supplier value chains to create best opportunities
Budgets	Project managers controls all aspects of the budget and limits access to financial records	Project manager operates an open book policy and shares financial responsibility and accountability with partners and other stakeholders
Personnel	Project manager gives orders and staff undertake tasks and project manager expedites the work	Project manager prepares and agrees clear terms of reference for staff and coaches personnel in delivering outcomes
Performance	Project manager maximizes efforts of individuals	Project manager agrees performance measures with staff and creates partnerships with suppliers and other stakeholders
Power	Project manager consolidates power and enforces rule	Project manager shares power and empowers individuals with responsibility for decision-making and facilitation

Figure 5.1 Model of collaborative involvement.

collaborative relationships there are certain prerequisites to fulfil; these include:

- addressing the organization's future (vision) and not its past
- building on its strengths while eradicating its weaknesses
- providing clear leadership and goals with a focus on results-oriented outcomes
- identifying the core values associated with these goals
- communicating the vision by focusing the attention of all involved
- celebrate accomplishments
- getting to know each other, listening to one another's stories and discovering one another's competencies and aspirations
- sharing information, insights, and key market trends which makes it possible to begin to spot new and exciting market opportunities

- understanding the issues, trends, and opportunities; so they can realistically evaluate the appropriateness and potential profitability of these items
- developing the appropriate teams and actively pursue the opportunities.

As you build up these key collaborative relationships with your partners, stakeholders, and customers, you can begin to ask a new set of questions. For example:

- How can we strengthen the competencies of our stakeholders, so that they become more successful in fulfilling their aspirations towards their customers?
- How can we combine our own competencies and those of our supplier/partners in unique ways so as to help our customers to become more successful?

The goal is to provide value added services within a context of ever changing business opportunities. To make this happen project management needs to build its core competencies (and organizational competencies) so that collaborations and teaming are second nature, a co-creative culture to better develop and build upon the talents of individuals.

5.2 Obstacles to stakeholder collaborations

Collaborative relationships can last a long time however, for some organizations they last only as long as the project, then they disappear or recombine in some new coalition for the next opportunity. The question here is, do we have project managers who can manage these situations with ease? Do project managers have the means to quickly spot and grow new opportunities?

When we form collaborations we are leveraging one another's knowledge as much, if not more so, than their financial assets, and clearly there are mutual benefits in doing so. There is, however, a school of thought that says the business of business is to make a profit for the shareholders and some managers do not always greet collaborations with open arms.

Obstacles to successful collaborations come in many guises some of these obstacles include perceived differences in:

- financial support
- business risk

- management capability
- opportunities for remuneration
- staffing projects
- reporting structures
- management support
- ethical policies
- regulatory policies
- management practices
- risk reward strategies
- reporting methods
- technical understanding
- career opportunities
- approach and flexibility
- stakeholder commitment
- perceptions
- decision-making policy.

With respect to the latter two points when collaborations do fail it is some times perceived that business decisions are taken behind close doors and in a secretive manner, and that the lack of adequate disclosure to either party is "one cause" for many a failed project. To be fair, reality may in some ways differ from perception. But in "our" profession, we follow the rule that perception is reality as far as stakeholders and shareholders are concerned.

5.2.1 Removing potential obstacles

When attempting to remove obstacles it should be remembered that removing obstacles will not necessary result in a successful project. What it may do is reduce the risk of it failing altogether. Experienced project managers that have worked on collaborative projects expect to encounter some of the above obstacles on a week-by-week basis. For example, those methodologies described in Section 1.1.1 include structured forms to monitor progress and future obstacles and other issues that arise during the project's life cycle.

At a strategic level we can cluster those obstacles listed above under three headings, namely type of company and size, structure, and performance:

1. *Company and size:* Collaborations often depend upon the size of the company and the functions and expertise within the

individual business units. This is often characterized by whether the company is centralized or decentralized in its capability and decision-making processes.

2. *Structure (centralized vs. decentralized):* The centralized structure is a traditional hierarchical approach. The central project office is the decision-making authority. Project operations are carried out under the direct supervision of central project office administration. The role of the central project office is that of central decision-maker and controller of the resources and workload. The centralized structure appears to operate effectively in facilitating communication of one team, one mission, and one goal. However, this structure is less flexible in responding to changes in workload and resources.

The decentralized structure, on the other hand, relies heavily on downward delegation of decision-making authority and autonomy. The role of the project office is that of monitor, and provider of technical assistance and administrator of policy. Given the diversity of operational structures, piloting different ideas simultaneously across a decentralized structure is not only possible, but also highly likely at any given time. However, variations in project operations make communication across office units in this type of structure much more challenging than in a centralized organization. This communication gap can often impose both operational variability and process implementation barriers across projects.

3. *Performance:* There are many ways to measure project performance in an organization. The most widely accepted approach is to monitor and measure deadlines (or milestones) through evaluating and interpreting the data that relate to the specific project deliverables. Because these data are used to measure deliverables, they are referred to as performance measures and/or indicators. Service performance indicators involve measuring the effectiveness, capability, and efficiency of the project.

Collecting appropriate data as performance indicators means understanding your project deliverables and comparing your project data against measures. It is important to use output from performance indicators to establish strategic goals. Performance indicators are not merely about counting the number of tasks, each project member completes; they are about evaluating the results of how that task was completed and the value added and by which contributor.

5.3 Collaborative stakeholder strategies

Some project organizations acknowledge the importance of including stakeholders in their policy and strategic development processes, however some do not. In my experience successful implementation of collaborative stakeholder strategies and supporting processes requires a change in thinking that looks for long-term solutions that are carefully arrived through stakeholder consultation. In developing collaborative strategies, the project organization needs to consider that each stakeholder has the ability to both threaten and co-operate, the objective is to reduce the threatening element and increase the co-operative behaviour of the stakeholder. In putting together collaborative stakeholder strategies we have to consider the:

- history and relationships among the stakeholder and partner organization
- substantive issues important to the stakeholder and partner organization
- stakeholder and partner organization underlying interests
- timing limitations or constraints affecting participation in the strategic process
- perceptions about any barriers to collaborative strategies
- stakeholders available alternatives to a collaborative strategy
- stakeholders level of commitment to a collaborative strategy and willingness to commit until the process is complete
- need to select appropriate stakeholder representative to participate in the strategic process.

As previously stated when developing collaborative strategies, it is important to examine not only strategies that tackle stakeholders who are positively willing to support the project but those who are negatively disposed towards the project as well. Some strategies may only be appropriate for stakeholders with a specific disposition towards the project, whether, *positive or negative*. In other cases a given strategy may be appropriate for both types.

Stakeholder strategies could be viewed as a problem-solving approach by which the project manager makes decisions and takes actions in order to satisfy a given need.

A stakeholder strategy results from reviewing both internal and external environmental influences. Internal influences would include the organizations strengths and weaknesses. Other

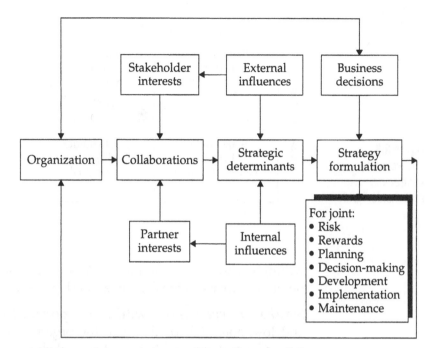

Figure 5.2
Strategic
formulation model.

influences would include the broader behaviour and cultural differences between stakeholder groups. See Figure 5.2.

There are at least three benefits to applying the strategic formulation model in business relationships. Firstly, it is a good description of the various entities involved. Secondly, it is a more useful view because it can be used to establish the active connections between the entities. Lastly, it identifies the stakeholder interest in the organization regardless of whether the business organization has any interest in them at all. The stakeholder model provides business management with a methodology for identifying all the groups affected by business decisions and their legitimate concerns, and for analysing the means by which these groups in turn can affect the interests of the organization. It thus provides a broad basis for evaluating project decisions. It also provides every stakeholder with a broad view of all other stakeholders capable of influencing the project.

5.3.1 The Polonsky stakeholder grid

Building on the work of Freeman (1984) and Savage (1991) Polonsky devised a strategic grid that maps five types of stakeholder strategy. These are: mixed blessing, supportive, non-supportive, marginal, and bridging. The grid suggested by Polonsky aims to position stakeholders within two domains those that are

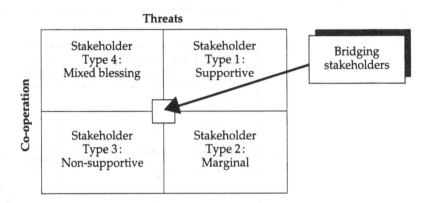

Figure 5.3
The Polonsky
strategic
stakeholder grid.

willing to co-operate and those that wont and so are considered potential threats to the organization (Figure 5.3).

Stakeholder Type 1 is one with a high potential for co-operation and low potential for threat to the organization. The strategy here is for management to have these stakeholders highly *involved.* In the case of the dumping, business management would want trade officials, legislators from the district where factories are located, employees whose jobs are threatened, domestic suppliers whose business would be negatively impacted, and others having a high potential for co-operation and a low potential threat. These groups will be supportive of the firm.

Stakeholder Type 2 is one with a low potential for co-operation and a low potential for threat. The appropriate management strategy here would be to have the stakeholder closely monitored for change in attitude. These stakeholders include consumer interest groups, local universities, environmental groups, and public affairs groups. A public affairs group may be concerned with the country's independent foreign sources of supply and may take a position, but the specific dumping case may not be of sufficient interest. *Monitoring* the situation would be appropriate.

Stakeholder Type 3 is one with a high potential for threat and a low potential for co-operation. The non-supporting groups could include academic economists, "free trade" public affairs groups, other industries trading heavily with the offending foreign firms, and others. The appropriate action is for the organization to actively defend its position.

Stakeholder Type 4 is one with a high potential for threat and a high potential for co-operation. This is a mixed-blessing type of

Type	Strategic view	Potential strategy
Mixed blessing	**High threat/high co-operation** These stakeholders are extremely important, for they have the ability to co-operate with the project or threaten the achievement of the project objectives.	**Collaborate with them** One appropriate strategy for mixed blessing stakeholders is to integrate them into the project strategy development process. This will ensure that the objectives of the stakeholders are included in strategy as it is formed and thus will not require a later "redevelopment" of strategy.
Supportive	**Low threat/high co-operation** These stakeholders have the ability to co-operate with the project, but have little ability to threaten its activities.	**Involve them** Use collaborative strategies. Using a collaborative strategy minimizes the potential for threatening behaviour and increases its co-operative behaviour.
Non-supportive	**High threat/low co-operation** These stakeholders have the ability to threaten the project activities, but have little ability to co-operative with the project organization. Governmental bodies are often considered to be non-supportive stakeholders.	**Defend against them** This group may require extremely innovative strategies to be developed in order to diffuse negatively disposed stakeholders within the group.
Marginal	**Low threat/low co-operation** These stakeholders have little ability to threaten the project activities or to co-operative with the project. This group may have little interest in the project activities at a given point in time.	**Monitor them** Interest may change over time and therefore the potential for co-operation or threat may change. Under such circumstances a collaborative and monitoring strategy minimizes the potential for threatening behaviour.
Bridging	One definition of the term bridging stakeholders is all groups who forward their own ends as well as to serve as links between other stakeholders.	One positive strategy would be to have open communication channels with the bridging stakeholders. This would allow projects to "influence" the bridging group's actions and therefore indirectly affect the "influenced" groups' expectations or behaviour towards the project itself.

Figure 5.4 Stakeholder strategies (modified for projects) after Polonsky (1995).

stakeholder. Management's handling of this type can make the firm either a success or a failure. For example, such a stakeholder in this case would be a computer chip maker's customers and defence officials. If either of the above believe that the level of higher quality produced by foreign firms and their very low prices are sufficient incentive to not press any dumping case then the anti-dumping action may not succeed. The strategy here is to collaborate. By collaborating, the stakeholder will remain actively co-operative and the firm will be able to influence the final position of the stakeholder.

Each strategy is not mutually exclusive; some are appropriate for more than one type of stakeholder group. For example, strategies designed to address *bridging stakeholders* are more complex than those of the other four groups. The organization must identify in which of the four quadrants the stakeholder falls, as well as identify which stakeholders can be affected by a bridging group and how important that bridging groups influence might be. One of the positive strategy approaches would be to have open communication channels with the bridging stakeholders. This would hopefully allow organizations to "influence" the bridging group's actions and therefore indirectly affect the "influenced" groups' expectations or behaviour towards the organization (Polonsky, 1995, p. 10). Figure 5.4 provides one view of each of the five alternative stakeholder strategies offered.

5.4 Stakeholder recognition and reward systems

As discussed the motives of each stakeholder will vary with their interest or claim on the project. For example the investor requires a total return of dividends, plus share appreciation that is satisfactory. Government, depending on the department, requires implementation of a public policy goal. Interest groups representing the NHS expect a better record of patient care, and so on. Those project managers that expect them can measure these diverse motives. The rewards, of course, vary as well, and are closely tied to the identity of the stakeholder.

As we learned in Chapters 2 and 3, stakeholder interests can be related to their degree of support for the organization, and is generally cemented in the early stages of the project. At the initiation and planning phases of a project, the project manager needs to gauge their potential to contribute to the longer-term strategic goals of the project. Experience would suggest that stakeholders are usually content to agree to "short-term" objectives and milestones, but are sometimes reluctant to agree to "longer-term" objectives and milestones without some form of inducement or incentive.

The strategic planning phase of a project is the most appropriate point in which to consider building complementary rewards systems that are tied to the project deliverables that deliver both on economic gain and emotional benefits to the stakeholders. Projects are usually divided into shorter periods and the end of each period is called a milestone. At milestones we recognize the results of our performance, evaluate them, and adjust our original plans if needed. At the completion of each milestone, we should, evaluate our attainments and assess the benefits and where appropriate reward our stakeholders.

One way of approaching a choice of reward strategy for stakeholders is to consider the amount of benefits to be achieved by the use of one or more stakeholder strategies and the costs to obtain them. As the greater number and intensity of strategies is applied, the benefits to be gained from the actions will increase to a point and then diminish. On the other hand, the costs, which will start at a low point, will increase as more effort takes place and more strategies are applied. The result is a point where the marginal costs exceed the marginal benefits. If marginal costs and marginal benefits are compared, it is clear that the actions taken will be balanced at one value.

5.4.1 Management by objectives

A well-known acronym among business organizations is MBO, meaning management by objectives. The concept of management by objectives includes several important determinants. *First*, it is the definition and specification of objectives – clarity, reality, measurability, and capability of evaluation. *Second*, it is the participants of objectives that are participation of managerial and non-managerial structures of employees in objective determination and achievement. *Third*, it is the time limit of objectives – to anticipate periods and fix time limits of the objective-attaining processes and activities concerning the relation between the objectives of employees and the objectives of the enterprise. *Fourth*, to provide feedback performances to design a communication system that would enable adequate support of feedback performances to the control, analysis, and corrections of objective-at-training activities and processes. *Fifth*, it is the stimulation to use economic and non-economic means and principles of motivation in creating organizational behaviour, that is the behaviour motivated by objectives to be achieved. See Figure 5.5.

The linking of stakeholder reward systems to projects objectives (or wider organization objectives) is a good way of accruing benefits that can be shared and passed directly to the bottom line of the balance sheet. For certain the choice of (which) project

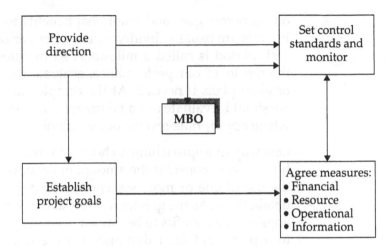

Figure 5.5
MBO framework.

objectives will be influenced by wider programmes within the organization, but may include some or all of the factors below:

- Specialization (degree of division of labour)
- Complexity (number of activities or subsystems – vertical, horizontal, and spatial)
- Hierarchy of authority (who reports to whom and span of control)
- Formalization (amount of written documentation)
- Standardization (degree similar work is done in uniform manner)
- Centralization (hierarchical level with decision-making power)
- Personnel configuration (deployment, e.g. administration, clerical, and professional : staff ratio).

For a project and stakeholder reward system to become truly part of an MBO plan, it must be stated in terms that are tangible and measurable, such as pounds, per deliverable or other countable benchmarks. Sometimes an objective is so obtuse that it is virtually impossible to define it in countable terms. In this instance, the objective should be broken down into a series of tasks that, upon their completion, become accountable benchmarks. A few questions the project manager should ask himself is: *what needs to be done to make a visible difference in the project and who benefits and why?*

The implementation of the MBO process requires a written plan because the function of writing requires the project manager to develop succinct, logical statements. Once written, the document can be referred to later for comparison, and there is no misunderstanding of the original statement, for being written, it has not changed through remembrance. Nor does the plan go away, for having been set in concrete, it is there for all to see, both the parties to the goal, as well as interested or related outside observers. In structuring the plan remember to:

- Link the stakeholder's performance to the objective.
- Establish meaningful, task-related, observable, measurable, and fair performance criteria.
- Factor in fixed and variable stakeholder costs.
- Prepare for the implementation by outlining the key points you want to cover with the stakeholders.
- Invite the stakeholder to provide an evaluation of his/her own performance based on the agreed criteria.
- Focus on behaviours, actions, and results.
- Avoid surprises (for either the stakeholder or the project owner).
- Plan for the future. Smart project managers spend about 20% of a performance review discussing past performance and 80% developing goals, objectives, and a plan for improving performance in the future.

5.5 Opportunity and stakeholder costs

All organizations and the projects done within them are undertaken within an environment of restricted resources that are generally allocated through various screening mechanisms.

All experienced project managers know that there is no such thing as a free lunch and as such we have to make choices about where we invest our time, energy, and cash. Although we anticipate making a net benefit from our project investments there is of course no guarantee. With this in mind the stakeholder processes of identify, attract, involve, maintain, release, and review require resources (cash and people) to manage them and stakeholder management is to some degree an opportunity cost. At the start of every project (or even before) the project manager should ask himself a question – *if we do not invest in our stakeholders what will be the consequences?*

The consequences some of which we have already touched upon in previous chapters can be summarized in two words "lost opportunity". The basic idea of opportunity is that for any choice you make, any action you undertake, you are giving up some other choice or action you could have done instead and that best alternative is the opportunity of the choice you made.

In other words, there is always an opportunity cost decision made when stakeholder choices are determined.

Economists argue that our main concern in wealth creation is not so much the (stakeholder) choices we make but the monetary effect of those choices. That is to say, what does a purchasing decision we make now really cost us in terms of future pounds? Knowing this information may make a difference in our decision-making process. While not wishing to contradict myself, while this statement is certainly true not all investments have a tangible outcome as Albert Einstein noted "not everything that can be counted counts, and not everything that counts can be counted". A point we will further explore in Chapter 6.

5.5.1 Stakeholder costs

Figure 5.6 provides a breakdown of the various types of cost known and used within classical accounting regimes. In defining which stakeholder cost estimates to incorporate into your plan I would recommend including those "fixed and variable" costs associated with each element of the stakeholder process.

Costs	Explanation
Opportunity	The cost of the next best alternative – if we spend on this what is the value of the foregone alternative. *Note*: correct "economic decision-making" uses opportunity cost measures. But from an accounting and tax standpoint we must also use historical costs in making decisions
Historical	The costs that the firm actually paid for the input or resource. This may be very different from the opportunity cost due to appreciation or depreciation in the value of the asset.
Fixed	Do not vary with the level of output; variable costs vary only because the output varies. *Note*: fixed cost are constant, variable costs are zero at zero output, and positive at other levels.
Variable	These are the avoidable costs, the cost incurred because activity is taking place.
Explicit	External payments made for normal company operations-payroll, electricity, etc.
Implicit	Cost that measure the value of the resources owned by the firm-owners time, financial capital invested, etc.
Note: all cost considerations should include both "explicit and implicit" cost, especially in the determination of the profitability of the enterprise.	

Figure 5.6 Types of cost.

An example is given in Figure 5.7. When putting together your stakeholder cost estimates there are some good practices to follow:

- Avoid "corridor" or unsure estimates
- Do not inflate estimates "to be on the safe side"
- Ensure that those in the right domain prepare their estimates

Stakeholder process	Examples of fixed costs	Examples of variable costs
Identify	• Employment 1. Wages 2. National insurance 3. Sick pay, etc. • Accommodation • Equipment	• Marketing • Advertising • Meetings • Lobbying • Travelling expenses
Attract	• Employment 1. Wages 2. National insurance 3. Sick pay, etc. • Accommodation • Equipment	• Interviewing • Specialist documentation • Contract • Meetings • Workshops/presentations • Travelling expenses
Involve	• Employment 1. Wages 2. National insurance 3. Sick pay, etc. • Accommodation • Equipment • Specialist training	• Travelling expenses • Catering expenses • Special payments for example, bonuses • General training • Meetings • Workshops/presentations • Specialist documentation
Maintain	• Employment 1. Wages 2. National insurance 3. Sick pay, etc. • Accommodation • Equipment • Specialist training	• Travelling expenses • Catering expenses • Special payments for example bonuses • Penalty payments • Meetings • Workshops/presentations • Specialist documentation
Release	• Employment 1. Wages 2. National insurance 3. Sick pay, etc. • Accommodation • Equipment	• Exit interviews • Specialist reports • Knowledge transfer • Bonus payments • Penalty payments
Review	• Employment 1. Wages 2. National insurance 3. Sick pay, etc. • Accommodation • Equipment	• Closure reports • Knowledge transfer • Archiving documents

Figure 5.7 Stakeholder costs.

- Ensure that those who will be working on the project prepare their estimates
- Work with the project triangle and assess trade offs
- Be careful of managers who push you lower budgets. This may compromise the functions of the product
- Costing should only be completed when the project and product are fully scoped
- Apply several costing methods to verify costing
- Use research to get independent estimates: acquire quotations from suppliers or the market, search the web
- Apply risk analysis on uncertain costs or on high cost activities
- Try to convert "intangible" costs to more "tangible" estimates
- Try to synchronize the individual cost estimates with the estimates made for the whole project as they tend to be tied to one another.

To monitor and control costs you will need to capture data and information from a variety of sources. Sources of information will include:

- time sheets
- cash receipts
- supplier invoices
- purchase orders
- expense forms
- payment slips.

For accounting purposes each source document must include the date, the amount, and a description of the transaction and the name and address of the party involved in the transaction. All source documents must be kept on file until the project is complete and thereafter archived for future reference in line with the organizations policy on archiving.

5.6 Chapter summary – 10 key points

The most important points to take away from this chapter are as follows. Remember:

1. collaborative stakeholder relationships to some extent have a basis in utilitarianism in that we seek the greatest good for the greatest number
2. organizations are sensitive to changing political, economic, and social and cultural trends
3. principles affect our view of the future and about other people, and ultimately our willingness to commit to our responsibilities

4. as you build up these key collaborative relationships with your partners, stakeholders, and customers, you can begin to ask a new set of questions

5. performance indicators are not merely about counting the number of tasks, each project member completes; they are about evaluating the results of how that task was completed and the value added and by which contributor

6. stakeholder strategies could be viewed as problem-solving approaches by which the project manager makes decisions and takes actions in order to satisfy given needs

7. in developing collaborative strategies, the project organization needs to consider that each stakeholder has the ability to both threaten and co-operate, the objective is to reduce the threatening element and increase the co-operative behaviour of the stakeholder

8. that stakeholders are usually content to agree to short-term objectives and milestones, but are sometimes reluctant to agree to long-term objectives and milestones without some form of inducement or incentive

9. for any stakeholder reward system to become part of a management by objectives plan, it must be stated in terms that are tangible and measurable, deliverables or other countable benchmarks

10. the basic idea of opportunity is that for any choice you make, any action you undertake, you are giving up some other choice or action you could have done instead and that the best alternative is the opportunity of the choice you made.

Chapter reading

Drucker, P. (1988) Management and the worlds work, Harvard Business Review, 66, 65–76.

Freeman, R.E. (1984) Strategic Management: A Stakeholder Approach. Massachusetts, Pitman Publishing Company.

Polonsky, M.J. (1995) Incorporating the natural environment in corporate strategy: a stakeholder approach. The Journal of Business Strategies, 12(2), University of Newcastle, Newcastle, Australia.

Savage, G.T., T.W. Nix, C.J. Whitehead, and J.D. Blair (1991) Strategies for assessing and managing organisational stakeholders. Academy of Management Executive, 5(2), 61–75.

Senge, P. (1990) The Fifth Discipline: The Art and Practice of the Learning Organization. New York, Doubleday.

6 A Framework for Analysing and Evaluating Stakeholder's Performance

6.1 Establishing project boards and review committees

In Chapter 2 (Section 2.1.2), we reviewed some of the key project roles and the responsibilities that go with these roles within the PRINCE2 framework. The concept of a *project board* was also introduced and its function within a project.

Some practitioners make a clear distinction between project boards and steering committees. I do not, because in practice they tend to be one and the same entity.

The composition and reporting line of this project board will be totally dependent on the nature of the project and the structure of the organization; however it is possible to draw some good practice lessons from my own projects. First keep it small – between six and ten people. This committee should not be the device for securing commitment across the organization (although it can be used for communication purposes) – this needs to be done by the process itself not by a committee. Depending on the size of the project this project board, should meet at least once a month, and provide direction and oversight to the project manager. It should review the status and plans of each group within the project. This project board should have the responsibility for adjusting priorities and reallocating budgets, when necessary. The chair of the project board is very important. The appointee should be someone who is a driving force behind the project and has the communication channel to top-level management. The other members of the committee will depend on the structure of the organization; it may not be necessary to have all interest groups represented as long as there is an adequate spread of types of interest – particularly as the numbers should be kept below 10.

Primary stakeholders Department of health representative Chief executive of trust Director of projects or informatics Senior clinicians
Secondary stakeholders Hospital personnel (nurses, doctors, etc.) Private sector providers Union representatives Trust public relations representatives
External stakeholders Technical advisors Pressure groups Third party providers Local authority
Extended stakeholders Patients General pubic Voluntary agencies

Figure 6.1
NHS project board membership for large IT project over £30 million.

Each member should be interested, and knowledgeable, about the challenges and opportunities faced by the project. For example, in NHS-related software projects members of the project board are generally made up from "all-four" stakeholder groups: primary, secondary, external, and extended (see Section 2.2 and Figure 6.1).

Although it is sometimes useful to have more than one primary stakeholder on the project board these set of people tend to consist of those are actually involved in the project and are required and drive forward the development process; one of these people will be the project manager. In small projects, this will be one person, in larger projects it may be two or three people (although not necessarily full time); reporting to a programme manager. These project managers would be responsible for undertaking the tasks in the project and would report to the project board through the programme manager.

6.1.1 The project board

Following on from our discussion on project governance in Section 4.6.1, some large software organizations go to extraordinary lengths to lobby stakeholders who can influence the composition of a project board. Why? Large projects are generally delivered in years not months and it is in the early stages of the project that support from key project board members is essential.

In my experience project managers generally have little direct influence when it comes to deciding who sits on the project board, indirectly however, they can lobby key stakeholders and senior managers to influence which people get appointed. Appointments to project boards should be agreed before the project starts. Sometimes however, the final appointments are not made until the project as commenced and if this is the case it is likely to be for political reasons and usually involves some level of propaganda.

As discussed in previous chapters *politics* play a significant part in whether a project is deemed to be successful or not. The project has a duty of care to the project board and that duty of care extends to providing a full and open view of the project. Likewise the project board should be equally open and frank with the project manager on what decisions it makes and why?

6.1.2 Project board decisions

Matters on which project boards will wish to make decisions are likely to include those associated with:

- Changes to the project scope in time, cost, or quality, which might need to be made in order to ensure that a project is delivered and exactly what this means in terms of usability and stakeholder expectations
- How the project can be delivered or further improved without significant extra funds being made available
- What additional (or different) arrangements need to be made to ensure delivery of the project
- Whether, and if so to what extent, provision should be made to enable the project to go ahead under different terms of reference
- What is needed in order to meet the expectations of the project stakeholders
- What (imaginative) ways can be found for addressing (or at least ameliorating) problems arising from shortages of resources? For example, space, people, etc.
- The full implications of any development of modularity, with its consequences for design and subsequent release

- What guidelines or policies there should be, if any, on consistency of management style covering, for example, on governance issues
- What advantages should be taken of the opportunities now (or likely to be) available as a result of developments in legislation that effects the project.

6.1.3 A working model

The Figure 6.2 defines a generic operating framework in which the project board operates. This generic framework is based on a number of components that together contain the most appropriate structure for software projects. These components are:

1. unit composition
2. situation
3. information needs
4. roles and responsibilities
5. execution
6. monitor and review.

1. *Unit composition:* the scope, terms of reference, approach, and leading individuals for the development of the project (in terms both of doing and of deciding).
2. *Situation:* a clear understanding of the intended overall direction of the project and of the challenges facing it; the opportunities presented by the emerging technologies and the environmental context within which the project will be working.
3. *Information needs:* the range of (shared) information within scope of the project; an analysis of the information items with the standards required for each requirements for an information infrastructure, and any gaps and problems.

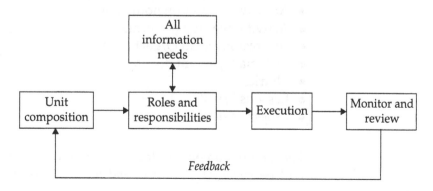

Figure 6.2
Project board
generic operating
framework.

4. *Roles and responsibilities:* identification of those (individuals) with any direct responsibilities for the creation or use of information; an understanding and acceptance as to what are their roles and responsibilities within the committee.

5. *Execution:* a priority list of tasks (with options) to be undertaken, projects, management plans against which to check progress programmes of change management to spread the project and gain acceptance and understanding of it.

6. *Monitoring and review:* monitoring the effectiveness of the project, monitoring the risks within the project and make recommendations to reduce any such risks.

6.2 Measuring contribution and performance

For any project board to undertake its role effectively it requires regular updates and reports from the project manager. If PRINCE2 is in use then the most likely reports generated will be *highlight and exception* reports.

In undertaking any software project it is prudent to provide the project board and each stakeholder with a copy of the project initiation document (or PID) although PIDs vary in structure and quality they should contain a section on how the project will report its progress and to whom. The following are typical sections that may be included in the PID:

- Highlight reports
- Change requests
- Project exception reports
- Changes in time/cost/functions
- Issues register
- Resource assignments and changes
- Activity completion notifications
- Activity overdue notifications
- Test results on all QA activities
- Risk management documents
- Metrics
- Lessons learnt
- Project review.

The PID document contains information on "how" the project will be *managed, measured, and monitored* until concluded. The

PID should also include adequate measurement in each of these following categories or group:

1. The effectiveness of project management
2. The effectiveness of stakeholder management
3. The effectiveness of the resources in use
4. The effectiveness of the risk process in use
5. The provision of a basis for future estimation of cost, quality, and schedule and risk. See also discussion in Section 5.4.1.

Any measurements should be sufficiently broad based and data should be collected for each situation to provide insight into the categories 1–4. To use metrics effectively, thresholds need to be established for those metrics. These thresholds should be estimated initially using local or known norms for various project classes. Specific project thresholds will evolve over time, based upon experience. Violation of a threshold value should trigger further analysis and decision-making. Continuous data on schedule, risks, effort expenditures, and other measures of progress should be available to the project board and all project personnel along with the latest revision of project plans.

6.2.1 Critical success factors

One of the most precious resources a project manager expends is his or her own time, and therefore their time must be focused on activities truly critical to the success of the project and not wasted on activities which are not critical to success. Collecting, processing, and validating data is costly and a time-consuming activity. So, in defining what attributes to measure within each of the stated categories it is practical to define those critical success factors (CSF) that allow the project board to make well informed decisions and judgements.

Generally speaking the larger and more complex the project the more complex the integration decisions related to the various project elements. The mass of data surrounding the activities becomes, in many cases, overwhelming, making it increasingly difficult to separate the critical from the less than critical. By involving the project board (and its stakeholders) in the CSF analysis, and iterating on this process at periodic intervals, the project manager will be able to focus on those activities of critical importance to project success and incorporate these results into the various elements of the project management process, thus providing him or herself with the underlying foundation essential to management planning and execution success.

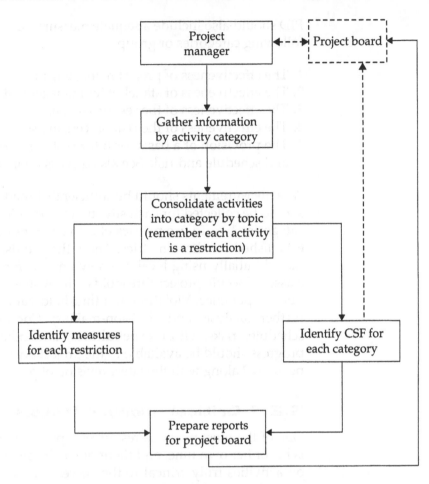

Figure 6.3
The CSF process.

A natural extension of CSF to the general field of stakeholder management will be a formal methodology for determining which data and measures are necessary for inclusion in the project information systems used by the project manager throughout the life of a project. The information needs will be specific to each project, and responsive to the individual needs of the managers, but will force consideration of issues whose scope is necessarily strategic. This will require that the project information system data provided to the project manager be as dynamic as are the CSF and measures on which it should be based. In spite of the unique nature of the information itself for each project, the overall use of CSF is general and therefore can be applied to any project (see Figure 6.3).

6.2.2 The balance score card approach

In Section 5.5 it was suggested "not everything that can be counted counts, and not everything that counts can be counted".

Although it is perhaps desirable to have measures for all your project activities there are occasions when this is not practical or even desirable. Some organizations that operate within the global software industry have started to incorporate qualitative processes into their measurement systems. One such reporting method that combines both qualitative and quantitative aspects is the balance score card (BSC). This BSC acknowledges the expectorations of different stakeholders and relates choice of performance to those strategic attributes of the project and is totally compatible with the CSF method previously described.

The BSC has its origins in the work undertaken by Kaplan and Norton (1992) in the early 1990s and was aimed at developing alternatives to purely financial-based performance measures. Kaplan and Norton compare the balanced scorecard to the dials and indicators in an airplane cockpit. For the complex task of flying an airplane, pilots need detailed information about fuel, air speed, altitude, bearing, and other indicators that summarize the current and predicted environment. Reliance on one instrument can be fatal. Similarly, the complexity of managing an organization requires that managers be able to view performance in several areas simultaneously. A balanced scorecard – or a balanced set of measures – provides that valuable information. The underlying philosophy of the method includes:

- the importance of clear communication of goals and priorities
- the benefits of learning and team working
- the importance of stakeholders.

BSC embraces both strategic (long-term) and operational measures. Importantly, performance is linked not only to short-term project goals but also to the way in which operational processes are managed for example, the processes of continuous improvement, innovation, and learning which are crucial to project success (Scheibeler, 2001).

In developing the BSC track progress against agreed targets. Targets should be based on the statements that define the state of the project at some future point. The content of the BSC should be continuously updated periodically taking into account learning experiences, causal assumptions, and shifts in priorities that have occurred due to changes in internal or external conditions experienced (see Figures 6.4 and 6.5).

BSC customer perspective	
CSF	**Measures**
Customer delivery performance • Results orientated • Responsive • Flexible adaptive • Price sensitive	• Response time to queries • Response time to action • Response time to changes • Response time to delivery • Cost to delivery • Cost to mitigate risk • Cost of contingency

Figure 6.4
Example BSC and CSF combined measure.

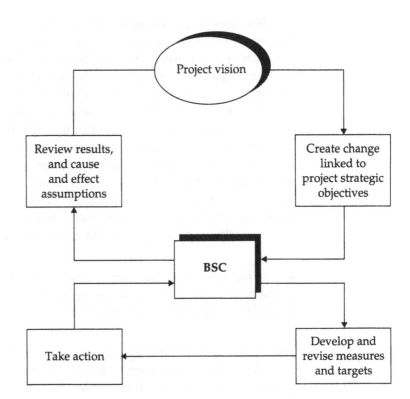

Figure 6.5
BSC mechanisms.

6.2.2.1 Using the BSC

Introducing the BSC as an alternative or supportive approach to measuring performance makes little sense if it is not used to trigger stakeholder action or changes in attitude or behaviour. For utmost effect the BSC should be used to form the centre of the project management system – if adopted in this way it will help to secure the strategic alignment of goals, initiatives, resources, processes, and systems throughout the project or wider organization if appropriate.

6.3 Qualifying risk and utilizing stakeholder's reviews

All software projects have an inherent amount of business, technical, and process risk. The degree of risk associated with each of these areas is dependent on the complexity of the project and the level of support the project has from its stakeholder and senior managers. We have already discussed some peripheral issues of risk and we have debated the problems associated with power and politics within projects and how stakeholders can have both a positive and negative influence on the outcome of a project.

In the context of this book the process of risk management deals with the concerns stakeholders have regarding the development of a software project. Risk management attempts to identify what could limit or prevent the creation of a system from achieving its functional and performance objectives within cost, quality, and schedule constraints. Such constraints might include:

- schedule
- resources
- budgets
- facilities
- contract
- dependencies
- customer
- contractors
- management
- vendors.

It is the responsibility of the project manager to undertake a baseline risk assessment to identify the potential risks to the project across the spectrum of development phases. Each of the identified risks should be analysed to determine the likelihood that the risk will occur and the impact if it does occur. The risks are then prioritized and sets of risk statements are produced in conjunction with stakeholders to be actively managed. Ideally, the baseline assessment is done during the planning phase of a software project, but the assessment techniques can be applied to an ongoing project.

Inputs to this risk process may include, but are not limited to the following:

- project business case
- project contract

- costs and resource budgets
- project metrics
- project functional and allocated requirements
- project task schedules
- previous risk management outputs
- previous project lessons learned
- list of potential business risks
- list of potential software development risks
- list of potential technical risks.

A continuous process of risk management reviews is then executed to reassess the status of identified risks, identify new risks, monitor the effectiveness of implemented risk reduction techniques, track the risks, and flag when contingency plans should be implemented.

One advantage of classifying risk into business, technical, and process is that the project manager can appoint stakeholders to be designated as the point of contact for issues related to each risk in that category. The nominated individual can then monitor their assigned risks and bring attention to the risk analysis group when the risk has changed status or has been encountered to a degree that will have a negative impact on the project. These nominated stakeholders should meet at regular intervals with the project manager to review the status of each risk.

6.3.1 Risk reviews

A good way of conducting risk reviews is to hold regular walkthroughs of your key risk statements with key stakeholders. The purpose of conducting walkthroughs is to discuss issues and spot errors of judgement as quickly and economically as possible. Generally speaking, it is more cost-effective to mitigate risk as early as possible, rather than waiting until a project phase has been finished and sent to the next step of development.

When consulting on any risk issue with your stakeholders, although you should be in listening mode, what they tell you will depend very much on how you pose the questions. Generally speaking, avoid imposing your own view of the issue, or inviting a particular response. It is good practice to ask questions differently to different stakeholders, and see if and how this alters the response. It is best not to presume that each stakeholder thinks about issues in the same way as you – they do not. Try to be responsive to and show respect for individual's attachment to established ways to control risks, particularly if you are proposing the possibility of significant change. Remember stakeholders often feel threatened by what they do not understand or know. Try to establish a dialogue with stakeholders rather than an exchange in which all received from you are standard statements and e-mails. Be aware of the limitations of different ways and ask stakeholders about their views.

Going back to the mechanics of holding walkthroughs a risk walkthrough is concerned with stepping through individual risk statements in an attempt to identify key issues with the objective of improving the delivery and quality of a particular project. Walkthroughs can be performed without any formal training or procedures; however, it is often the case that it helps to introduce some formalization or structure to the review process. As with any review, it is important to adopt the right attitude to a structured walkthrough. Specifically this requires commitment from both management and stakeholders to ensure:

- walkthroughs are scheduled in advance
- adequate time is allowed for a review
- the necessary stakeholders are available
- the review is effective.

Commitment is therefore required before, during, and after the walkthrough. And each statement must be updated together with all agreed actions at the close of the meeting.

A risk walkthrough can take place at virtually any point in the project. In general it is preferred to have the first walkthrough as early as possible, but not so early that the project is incomplete or contains many trivial risks that the project manager could have removed or mitigated them. The primary reason for avoiding a walkthrough at a late stage is that the project manager and his/her team may have invested so much of their time that he/she may be reluctant to make changes in the strategy. The project manager may also have needlessly wasted a lot of time detailing mitigation plans when the review team could have done it more quickly and economically if they had seen the strategy at an earlier point (McManus, 2004, p. 53).

When the group reaches consensus on what action to take the project manager should update the risk register and publish the content to all key personnel. The final activities in a risk analysis event are a presentation of the results and a meeting with the project board, at a minimum. It is recommended that the presentation be conducted as a formal presentation to all members

Issue	Risk	Mitigation statement
1. Multiple vendors/ contractors	Co-ordinating multiple vendors	Ensure adherence to standards, both technical and managerial. Emphasize the importance of regular status reporting.
2. Poor vendor support	Time wasted waiting for response to queries or due to rework arising from mistaken assumptions made by the project team in the interim	Impose contractual constraints/safeguards. Request documentation in advance. Ensure effective account manager. Identify a user group with other clients.
3. Critical dependence on external suppliers	May miss milestones waiting for deliverables	Ensure suppliers are aware of schedule commitment. Request interim status reports and review of partially complete deliverables so that the project team can verify the supplier's estimates of the effort to go. Impose contractual obligation.
4. Number of inter-project dependencies	Time wasted awaiting completion of other projects not within the project manager's control	Have a co-ordination project with the critical path specified in terms of projects. Recommend a strategic/architectural plan is produced.
5. Overlapping scope with other projects	Parallel, or duplicate, development of similar areas with different approaches causing confusion and irritation to the user	Establish cross-project standards to ensure consistency. Establish change control procedures to manage the different changes proposed by different systems. Recommend a strategic/architectural plan is produced.

Figure 6.6 Basic risk register – example of top five risks.

of the board. This presentation can be facilitated using power point slides. An example outline for the presentation appears below:

- Review of the risk assessment processes
- Complete database of risks with attributes
- Top five risks (see Figure 6.6)
- Documented contingency actions and a synopsis of each associated plan of action.

Key considerations here include having all participants attend and to conduct the presentation such that participants know what happened to "their" risks and to help determine risks that need to be raised with the project sponsor.

It is generally accepted practice to send out the risk register for review prior to issuing it as configuration document. The document should be distributed without prejudice. If the register is to go to third party providers it is generally accepted practice to obtain non-disclosure agreements first.

6.4 Contingency planning

In an effective project, work is planned out in advance. Planning means setting performance expectations and goals for groups and individuals to channel their efforts towards achieving project objectives. Getting stakeholders involved in the planning process will help them understand the goals of the project, what needs to be done, why it needs to be done, and how well it should be done.

All project plans contain critical elements. A critical element is a task assignment or responsibility of such importance that unacceptable performance in that element would result in a weakness that the projects overall performance is unacceptable. For example the production of:

- the requirements specification
- working standards
- the logical/physical system design
- the prototype
- the working model
- the prototype
- the test strategy
- the implementation strategy
- the training strategy.

Experienced project managers know that critical tasks such as those identified above are dependent on many variable actions and such actions are subject to unpredictability, which puts the project at greater risk. In any such situation the project manager must have a "contingency plan" or fall back position.

Whilst by no means exhaustive the essential elements of a contingency plan include: determining criticality, planned mitigation scenarios, contingency losses, contingency options, contingency costs, and trigger dates. Each of these elements should be included for each contingency that is linked to a critical task within the plan.

6.4.1 The process

The contingency planning process can be organized into three phases. The first is *pre-planning* and strategy development where objectives are defined, critical dependencies are determined, critical planning assumptions are made, responsibilities are defined, project management is instituted, and strategic parameters are defined.

The second phase, which is the *planning phase*, is the actual writing of the plan. A four-step contingency process is recommended. These steps are:

1. establish a contingency planning working group (include "your" stakeholders)
2. perform a contingency plan capability assessment (this is not a risk assessment)
3. establish contingency priorities
4. prepare programme for contingency.

The contingency plan, which should be developed using a template (Figure 6.7) and associated contingency planning, working group sessions, should primarily focus on this phase. As one project manager put it to me: *It is one case we have found that people will intuitively understand that contingency planning now is much less expensive than waiting to later, which also helps. The one vital thing is to get a team together that is able to represent all levels of the project, as the priorities of different individuals/business units are tremendously different and if not represented up front can skew the prioritization process.*

We find that workshops work really well, with invitations extended throughout the business. The dedicated team is usually very small, which is good anyway because people able to understand the real ramifications of continuity and contingency planning can be very expensive indeed.

Like all aspects of project management there is a cost to undertaking this exercise. In order to be able to make contingency planning cost-effective, the costs incurred must be compared to the potential damage and loss of productivity, and assessed accordingly. The following costs should be considered:

• Costs for compiling contingency plans
• Costs for executing the plan
• Costs for the restoration of the situation.

Project name	**RHR system**
Configuration reference Id	**CRC0012**
Project phase	**Logical design**
Value of this task (T9)	**£280,000**
Task Dependencies (*from main project plan*)	**T9** **D11, 15, 19, and 20**
Estimated completion date	**November 2004**
Monitoring frequency or trigger dates	**Weekly**
Most critical scenario and potential outcomes for schedule, quality, and cost. List assumptions made for each scenario. Impact of each scenario on specific business operations along with: 1. lists of critical elements 2. high-level estimates of financial and market implications 3. list of potential contingency options for avoiding or mitigating the impact of risk within the scenario.	
Contingency plan (and strategy) (*Define*)	
Personnel Effected (*Define roles and responsibilities*)	
Estimated costs to implement contingency plan and restore schedule (*Define*)	

Figure 6.7
Example of
contingency plan.

Contingency plans generally require the expenditure of all components of the budget once they are authorized. Unless they are triggered, event-driven contingencies require expenditures only for plan development and contingency preparations. A budget is necessary for contingency execution but this money should not be spent unless the contingency is initiated.

In the third phase, or *post-planning phase,* actions are carried out for testing, exercising, and training on the plan. The contingency plan should be a configuration item and reviewed and distributed at regular intervals. Although it is difficult to say how much time should be devoted to reviews my recommendation would be the equivalent of one man-day per month. A contingency plan must also take account of the interaction of other situations and of the respective contingency measure taken. For instance, missed or additional requirements can be controlled by means of a change request. However, the use of change requests can, in their turn, give rise to new threats, for example to resource commitments, access to specialist data architects, contract changes, etc.

A word of advice when building your contingency plans, you must be very careful not to build a contingency plan that is too dependant upon another project or individual, that impacts the project process, and the rest of the dependency chain. If you build your restoration plan that is dependant upon another project, or something "out-of-your-control", you will then need to build a contingency plan for the contingency plan. As you can imagine, this gets complicated. That is, it has that ripple effect. Those project managers that have experienced this will probably appreciate this better than those that have never been there.

The contingency plan should "not" be limited to one possible outcome; where practical it should include a combination of methods that complement one another to provide capability over the full project spectrum. A wide variety of contingency approaches should be considered; the appropriate choice depends on the severity of the situation and the projects contractual arrangements. Specific recovery methods may include renegotiating commercial contracts with clients, or reciprocal agreements with internal project or resourcing managers, or reviewing service level agreements with the equipment vendors.

Once the contingency plan has been finalized, project management should ensure that at least two people (one of which must be the project manager) in each affected area are familiar with the plan and are prepared to assume the responsibility of implementing the plan and directing other personnel, when needed.

6.4.2 Benefits of contingency planning

For the project and the project manager there are a number of benefits to undertaking contingency planning. These are summarized below:

- Presents a professional approach to the client and its stakeholders
- Provides the project board with a level of confidence
- Provides a means of correlating other related activities for example, risk analysis
- Provides a mechanism for reviewing the whole project
- Provides a mechanism for tracking critical tasks
- Prioritises responses in case of conflicts
- Ensures that issues are adequately covered in budgets and resource plans

- Enables quick reaction to resolve problems thereby reducing schedule down time
- Ensures the project is focused on achieving results (schedule, cost, and quality)
- Shortens the long lead times required for many contingencies (replacing a supplier may take more than a day)
- Ensures planning is conducted from both a top-down and a bottom-up perspective
- Ensures the contingency strategies are turned into specific, budgeted, assigned, and implemented contingency programmes
- Allows for policies and guidelines that govern the implementation of a selected strategy to be agreed up front with the project stakeholders
- Allows for financing contingency planning efforts at an early stage in the project
- Allows the project manager to offer incentives and measure risk/benefit.

6.5 Lessons learned (and peer appraisal)

When the project finishes a stage (or phase) it is good practice to hold a lessons learned session (or peer appraisal review) to gain valuable information and insight into what went right and what went badly and to allow stakeholders to have their say before leaving or rejoining the project. The best way to capture the information is in an open session where each participant can contribute in a neutral way. Information gained from these sessions should be retained for future reference – the most convenient and economic way of doing this is by creating a database. The information in your database could include:

- project ID
- subject category
- statement of lesson learned
- risk mitigated and not mitigated
- personnel involved and roles
- costs incurred
- recommendations implemented or not implemented (and why?)
- date the review was undertaken.

To conclude this chapter, I would like to revisit "some" of those key problem areas raised in Section 3.6, and some lessons learned starting with inadequate customer involvement.

133

6.5.1 Inadequate customer involvement

Using personnel from the customer/client organization is a must – in the early stages of the project it is vital that the project has the right balance of stakeholders with domain and technical knowledge. Involving people with pure systems knowledge is fine if such people have an in-depth understanding of the business process, however, many projects have a strategic angle, which is not always understood by technical stakeholders. Where this is the case evidence would suggest that the project is at risk.

6.5.2 Poorly defined scope of system

It is a frequently sited in many a project post-mortem that the project was ill-defined and suffered from severe scope creep. Evidence would suggest that where this was the case there were insufficient systems in place to track, measure, and communicate changes in requirements.

Poor configuration management is also seen as a key causal factor in why projects experience scope creep – poor traceability and lack of peer reviews are also seen as contributing reasons to failure. Successful projects allocate a significantly higher amount of resources to the requirements engineering phase than the average project (successful projects typically expend 25–30% on this activity).

6.5.3 Stakeholders do not know what they want

Projects are sometimes undertaken as a leap of faith in that they are started with no clear strategic vision of what is required, but powerful stakeholders throw their weight behind the project and it kicks-off (without too much objection). Later on, of course questions are asked about strategic alignment, who is paying, what are the benefits, etc. At this stage of course stakeholders are closing ranks and the project is looking sick and under threat of closure.

There must be a demonstrable connection between the project and business benefits aligned to a strategic vision. The focus or priority of the strategy should provide the direction and strategic objectives for the project. High-level statements are useful here in that they help management focus on the business objectives and goals of the project. It is important not to quibble over whether a particular statement becomes a goal or an objective.

What is important is to get issues on the table. Designating them can come later.

Remember to ask the question why are we doing this? The following example illustrates this point.

One NHS trust recently made a decision to replace the financial and human resource system, as it no longer met the long-term requirements of the trust. The financial system needed to be altered to match changes made to financial and accounting policies, practices, and reporting requirements. A new human resource system was needed because the current system could not provide:

- a single point of data entry
- a comprehensive and timely reporting
- integration with the financial applications.

In answering the question "what business benefit do we expect to achieve?" The trust expected business value to be achieved through the implementation of a fully integrated financial and human resource system would be as follows:

- Elimination or substantial reduction of the multiple interface or supplementary systems developed by organizations. This would reduce costs and improve efficiencies.
- Improvements in the accuracy and timeliness of information.
- More functionality than the previous systems provided.
- A system that is totally compliant.

6.5.4 Poor methodology and estimates

The Standish Group research shows that 53% of software projects cost 189% of their original estimates. Obtaining good estimates is a prerequisite – estimates will not lower costs but will improve the chances of delivering projects within the schedule constraints. There is evidence to suggest that a tried and tested estimating process aids business reputation.

According to members of the project and stakeholder community project negotiations are significantly enhanced when estimates are easily understood. For accomplished information systems project managers, estimates will become the basis for scope negotiation. In the absence of solid support for project estimates, I believe most software project managers will have few alternatives aside from acquiescing to unattainable expectorations.

From a cultural perspective, organizations must be prepared to walk away from a project rather than commit to unrealistic dates or budgets (McManus, 2003, p. 7).

6.5.5 Insufficient time allotted for user acceptance testing and training

The inability to get the support of users has long been a reason for software engineering project failure. Evidence suggests that where projects overrun their schedules by 10–15% testing is usually squeezed into unachievable time boxes.

If you are in this situation, you must face the reality that your system will fail and that some of your stakeholders (or users) will encounter problems. Work with business users to rank system-testing priorities to their business and begin testing the most important ones immediately. Schedule the remaining tests based on projected failure dates and importance. Determine which modules will not be tested in time, figure out how to circumvent resulting problems, and remove where applicable. Finally, work in the company of business users to establish contingency plans aimed at avoiding disruptions to their business operations.

6.5.5.1 User training

A common perception in delivering software projects is that application software, with its graphical user interface, requires little training of the user community, which in many instances is keen to make this application successful. The product is rolled out without aligning business processes or considering incentives for users, making it impossible to realize the full project business benefits.

So what is the message? The message is to get the training (and rollout) strategy agreed preferably after the design phase is concluded. Agree with your stakeholders/users what training is required and for who. Discuss and agree how the training will be delivered, monitored, and measured. It is helpful to users and other stakeholders to have training materials and schedules in advance of the sessions (my advice is 2 weeks before training commences). Some managers agree to undertake pilot sessions before the formal sessions commence primarily to gage the adequacy of the training to be provided. Running pilots in my experience is highly recommended.

In summing up this lessons learned section it is strongly recommended that you:

- Train stakeholders and internal customers in the project methodology.
- Requirements or exclusions: state clearly what is expected.
- Establish a stakeholder partnership for development and project management.
- Ensure a modelling language is used to express the requirements, which should be a disciplined and accepted technique. An example of a standard modelling language is the unified modelling language. The appropriate software tools should be used to express the requirements in such models.
- Take an iterative and incremental approach to requirements analysis.
- Hold formal and informal reviews of all project plans and other key documents.
- Write test cases against requirements and plan your test strategy up-front.
- Prioritize tasks using an evaluation framework.
- Subject all key documents to configuration management and effective change control.
- Develop and evaluate user interface prototypes for portions of the requirements that are not clearly understood.
- Ensure you have an agreed training strategy in place before commencing user acceptance testing.

6.6 Chapter summary – 10 key points

The most important points to take away from this chapter are as follows. Remember:

1. the project board should have the responsibility for adjusting priorities and reallocating budgets, when necessary.
2. generally have little direct influence when it comes to deciding who sits on the project board, indirectly however, they can lobby key stakeholders and senior managers to influence which people get appointed.
3. in undertaking any software project it is prudent to provide the project board and each stakeholder with a copy of the PID although PIDs vary in structure and quality they should contain a section on how the project will report its progress and to whom.

4. one of the most precious resources a project manager expends is his or her own time, and therefore their time must be focused on activities truly critical to the success of the project and not wasted on activities which are not critical to success.

5. although it is perhaps desirable to have measures for all your project activities there are occasions when this is not practical or even desirable.

6. targets should be based on statements that define the state of the project at some future point.

7. all software projects have an inherent amount of business, technical, and process risk. The degree of risk associated with each of these areas is dependent on the complexity of the project and the level of support the project has from its stakeholder and senior managers.

8. try to establish a dialogue with stakeholders rather than an exchange in which all received from you are standard statements and e-mails. Be aware of the limitations of different ways and ask stakeholders about their views.

9. in an effective project, work is planned out in advance. Planning means setting performance expectations and goals for groups and individuals to channel their efforts towards achieving project objectives.

10. contingency plans should "not" be limited to one possible outcome; where practical it should include a combination of methods that complement one another to provide capability over the full project spectrum.

Chapter reading

Kaplan, R. and D. Norton (1992) The balance score card: measures that drive performance. Harvard Business Review, 70(1), 71–79.

McManus, J. (2003) Information Systems Project Management, UK, FT Prentice Hall, Pearson Education, p. 7

McManus, J. (2004) Risk Management in Software Development Projects, Elsevier Butterworth-Heinemann, pp. 51–53.

Scheibeler, A. (2001) Balanced Scorecard for KMU, Berlin, Springer Verlag.

Selected Essays in Stakeholder Management

7.1 Essay No. 1: Software Stakeholder Management

(Its not all its coded up to be)

Quality software is typically defined as "defect-free" code. However, a more inclusive definition is meeting customer expectations, which is accomplished through applying a project stakeholder management model.

7.1.1 The project

It was time for the project team's unveiling of the new software system. A year had passed since they were first commissioned to develop a new order entry system. The project team was especially proud of the work they had done. They worked hard to make sure that the project was done on time, on budget, and performed exactly as they thought everyone said that it needed to function. "We finally did things right this time," said the project manager. Everyone was sent to the application's training class to learn how to use the new system. Today was the day for the new order entry system to be used by those who had been trained. On the other hand, the sales representatives did not understand why the order entry system had to change; the old one worked just fine. The first anxious sales representative sat down at the sophisticated new computer station to enter the first order, and said, "This is too complicated. I cannot use this!" Another sales representative picks up the rhetoric and says, "Yes, this will never do!" The Sales Department swells with groans of frustration. A concerned sales manager hears the complaints and thinks about all the money spent. The sales manager glares at the project manager and says, "This is not what I wanted! This will never do!" These are the very same people trained a month and a half ago. The project team feels betrayed. How could they do this to people who have worked so hard to get them what they wanted?

The story may be exaggerated (just a little), but have not we all heard of or been a part of a project like this in our lifetime? Unfortunately, some of us have been the user, the proud team member, the trainer, and yes, even the one that will take the fall – the project manager.

7.1.2 Project stakeholder process

This project manager failed to realize that not only she/he is responsible for delivering the software system, but is also responsible for managing stakeholder's expectations. Perhaps not even realizing who are software system's stakeholders is the first mistake. We must recognize that "software stakeholders" extend beyond just the user.

A formal project stakeholder process assists in the:

- identification of these stakeholders
- definition of their specific stake in the project
- development of a communication strategy to specifically address stakeholder interests
- prediction of stakeholder behaviour to analyse project impact
- adaptation of this strategy in the project implementation.

7.1.2.1 Identifying stakeholders

There are many "software stakeholders" to be identified for a project. To identify all of the current and potential stakeholders, let us examine how software quality might be characterized with respect to stakeholder expectations. A typical software quality attribute and expectation is the lack of defects. However, this is a very narrow view of software quality. A more comprehensive view is defined by IBM, which measures the ability of its software products to satisfy CUPRIMDSO quality attributes – capability, usability, performance, reliability, install ability, maintainability, documentation/information, service, and overall. Quality attributes such as these are what Juran called quality parameters for "fitness for use". Subsequently, a software product that was thoroughly tested and "bug free" may not meet current (or even future) stakeholder (customer) expectations, such as easy to use, short response time, and easy to change, resulting in dissatisfaction. Looking at this broader definition of software quality, the project manager in the project described can identify all of the "stakeholders" – the project team, the software supplier, the user department, and the IS Department Manager. Each of these stakeholders has a different reason for having an interest in the software system, which influences their behaviour. Management of these "stakeholder interests" is referred to as stakeholder management. While this is important in every project, it is especially important for software development where the deliverables are not as tangible as constructing a building.

7.1.2.2 Identify behavioural influences

Projects are developed in an organizational environment within a company, consisting of functional departments with organization goals and objectives. These goals and objectives evolve as the organization reacts to market and other environmental impacts. Project managers need to identify and interact with key organizations and individuals within the project systems environment. This management process is necessary to determine how the stakeholders are likely to react to project decisions, what influence their reaction will carry, and how they might interact with each other and the project manager to affect the chances for project success. The impact of project's strategy and decisions on all the stakeholders must be considered in any rational approach to the management of a project.

7.1.2.3 Develop a communication strategy

Once the stakeholders are identified and their interests understood, the most important activity as a project manager is to define the project goals, scope, and end results. While organizational goals may have initiated the project, these goals may not have considered all of the stakeholders. The project manager must revisit the project deliverables with all of the stakeholders, and process the information received from the stakeholders. This understanding must then be articulated back to the stakeholders to obtain definition and agreement. In all cases, this definition and agreement must be documented.

Not only are these goals, scope, and end results established at the start of a project, but they must also be communicated throughout the project life cycle. Again, a project is developed in a dynamic organizational environment. The project manager must manage stakeholder expectations by listening to current business needs, addressing any yet unstated stakeholder requirements, and adjusting project deliverables to address those needs. What was perceived as a need a year ago when the original goals and scope were defined may not be what is needed now. The project manager must also be sure that the project owner, the IS Manager in this case, is clear on project goals and objectives. The IS Manager can assist in managing business requirements, acquiring additional resources to meet changing needs, and breaking down organizational barriers to success. With clear goals and objectives, the project manager also can direct the project team towards the agreed upon requirements. Given the most talented people in the company on the project, the project team still cannot reach the goal without a clear target.

The goals and objectives must also be communicated to the end users of the software. In return, the project manager must listen to the needs and concerns of the users, and assure them that their concerns are understood. User "buy-in" is key to managing their expectations. Methods to obtaining user "buy-in" can include prototyping interfaces, and conducting training early in the design phase to solicit user feedback. Obviously the more the user interface differs from the current system, the more resistance that will be expressed by the user. It is important to keep this aspect in mind when developing the end user communication strategy, as it will mostly definitely impact their behaviour. If a software supplier is used, the project manager must also communicate goals and objectives to the supplier and make these parts of the contract. In need of special attention, but often overlooked is the contractual training to be provided. Often, training is conducted once after the design is mostly complete, which may be too late to accommodate specific needs. Typical training provided by the software supplier is a "show-and-tell" class, and may not address the users' deepest concerns, for instance "how will I use it on my job?" While a good introductory class, this type of "show-and-tell" class may present more questions for the users than answers, creating a stage for animosity. The project manager should use this opportunity to address concerns and specific "likes" and "dislikes" to build a communication channel and/or present actual user prototype screens as more focused alternative.

A second training class scheduled close to system startup should train users using actual examples. It has been my experience that the closer training is conducted to actual system startup, the more successful the startup. A few individuals may even need one-on-one training. Of course, user manuals as much as we like to keep them in the drawer should be part of the project as they also are part of the end user communication strategy, perhaps in the form of a quick reference written from the users' perspective. Of course, an ideal method of delivering user assistance would be an integrated online help, and throw away the manuals, but then this may not be cost-effective for smaller implementations. A widely distributed software application such as Microsoft Excel or Word would significantly benefit maintenance costs.

Thinking that all this training adds costs to the project? Yes, it does, however I have observed project after project which shortcuts training by not properly planning, and/or not soliciting user feedback costs 2–3 times their original estimate in the end (if there is an end). Without user "buy-in" throughout the project life cycle, users will find every reason not to use the system, and the project will incur unneeded costs just to ease their complaints.

7.1.2.4 Predict behaviour and adapt

Based on an understanding of stakeholder behavioural influences and a communication strategy, the project manager can proceed to predict stakeholder behaviour in executing a project. The project manager should study stakeholders with a high-vested interest carefully, and their strategies and actions noted to see what effect such actions might have on the project's outcome. Once the potential effect is determined, then the project execution should be modified through resource reallocation, replanning, or reprogramming to accommodate or counter the stakeholder's actions through the stakeholder management model. For example, perhaps the sales manager takes the attitude that the department is too busy to provide input in accepting project deliverables. Offer to have the project status meeting in the sales area, communicate the decisions that need only sales participation, and provide a meeting agenda with a timeframe. If a sales representative on the project team is not possible, then negotiate that yourself and/or a project team member observe a sales representative's different situations. It is important to establish a communication channel with the end user department to establish their project ownership.

7.1.2.5 Effective stakeholder management – stakeholder satisfaction

A formal stakeholder management process ensures that multi-year projects, which are subject to so much change, are adequately managed. The typical reliance on informal or hit-or-miss methods for obtaining stakeholder information is ineffective for managing the issues that can come out of any type of project. By developing a strategic management model for each project, the project manager has assembled adequate intelligence for the selection of realistic options in the management of stakeholders. The body of knowledge for the Certified Software Quality Engineer (CSQE) recognizes that delivering quality software that satisfies stakeholder expectations is contingent on successful project management. Not only is the project manager responsible for the project definition and execution, but the successful project manager also accepts the responsibility for stakeholder management. In order to satisfy stakeholder's expectations, their needs (stated and unstated) must be managed, and the ultimate responsibility is the project manager.

(This essay is credited to Robin Dudash of Innovative Quality Products and Systems Inc, and is reproduced with permission, Copyright IQPS, 2004.)

7.2 Essay No. 2: Stakeholder Management

Projects do not exist in isolation. Even if there is a defined brief, budget, programme and scope of works the project is still subject to external influences. The project exists within a "political" environment, populated by all those who have a particular stake or interest in the outcome of the project. This political environment and the expectations of stakeholders represent significant risk to a project. It is unlikely that the requirements of all stakeholders will coincide and they will seek to influence the project in order to meet their own requirements. Pressure from stakeholders generates change and change increases the complexity of the management task, jeopardizing cost, and programme certainty. However if the views of project stakeholders are not addressed and if stakeholders are not involved in the development of the project then the project is unlikely to deliver optimum value for all involved. It is important that project managers strike the right balance between stakeholder involvement and isolation of the project from external influence in order to achieve delivery on cost and time but also to maximize benefit for the client and his stakeholders.

7.2.1 Background and general principles

Stakeholders are those who have a stake or an interest in a project or strategy undertaken by a company or an organization, they will be affected in some way be the project and so have an interest in influencing it. They may benefit from the project and so will be supportive and positive about it; conversely, the project may damage their interests or they may perceive it will have a negative outcome for them and so they will seek to stop it or at the very least project it in a bad light.

In construction projects stakeholders can include:

- users of a building
- funders
- neighbours
- regulatory bodies
- general public.

It generally falls to the client to manage project stakeholders. In order to do this the client needs to reconcile the differing stakeholder requirements and pass clear direction to the project manager. Where briefing information is late, where answers to questions are delayed or where sign off of the design at different stages is a lengthy process this is probably because the client representative is liaising with the different project stakeholders in order to gain their agreement.

The term multi-headed client is often used to describe organizations where the decisions are not made by one individual but by a group. Some projects are the result of a joint venture between different organizations or development partners, this is common in the public sector, for example transport projects. For public projects or projects within large private organizations it is often the case that there are numerous internal stakeholders as well as external ones.

Stakeholder influence is often felt most keenly in the early stages of the project, the project is flexible at this stage and can be changed and stakeholders are generally aware of this. Once it starts to progress it takes on a momentum and a power of its own and the cost of stopping it or altering its direction becomes high. Stakeholder influence often drops off markedly when construction starts but will increase again as handover nears.

Project managers should continue to manage stakeholder expectations to ensure that the completed building meets the needs of stakeholders as well as possible and is favourably accepted.

Some clients are better at managing stakeholder influence than others, and some stakeholders are easier to manage than others. On a sizeable publicly funded project it is easy to identify 40–50 stakeholder groups all with different involvement, requirements, levels of power to influence the project, and levels of interest in doing so. This is a very complex situation to manage.

7.2.2 Internal and external stakeholders

7.2.2.1 Internal stakeholders

There are broadly two groups of project stakeholders, those internal and those external to the client organization. The type most usually recognized are the external stakeholders, however the management of internal stakeholders is often more problematic. In construction projects it is often difficult to identify who actually is the client, there may be a nominated single point of contact but this person is not really the "client" just the representative of the client organization. Very often it is the case that this person has the responsibility of juggling a whole range of different requirements within the client organization and as a result they will be subject to many influences, which will may well affect the project as change. Within the client organization there will be a whole range of individuals with very different "stakes" in the project, unless the nominated client representative takes a very strong line they will succeed in influencing the course of the project.

The client organization is made up of a whole range of individuals with differing wants and needs who make up a "multi-headed" client. In these situations the decision-making process becomes complex. Questions cannot be answered directly by the nominated client single point of contact. That single point of contact must negotiate with the various other stakeholders within the client organization in order to get an answer.

There is a school of thinking that states that organizations do not have goals, it is the individuals within the organization that use the organization to further their own differing personal goals. By extension of this, the individuals use the projects the organization undertakes to achieve their own ends. If we consider this: Do you go to work to help your company achieve every bullet point of its mission statement? Or do you get the 7 a.m. train every morning to earn money, gain experience, improve your curriculum vitae (CV), work on interesting projects, grow your department, build your empire, gain promotion, and be part of the team? The same applies to the people in your client's organization.

It is hardly surprising that when you are building to meet the diverse goals of your multi-headed client, it is difficult to find the right solution that satisfies the goals of most of those individuals and prevents those who do not get exactly what they want from obstructing the project.

Internal stakeholders could be anyone within the organization. Most commonly, they are the eventual users of the project, but they could also be the heads of marketing, IT or human resources, other employees, trade unions, and so on. All have a stake in the project and all can affect it, directly or by influence.

7.2.2.2 External stakeholders

External stakeholders are the individuals or organizations who are not part of the client organization but nevertheless have an interest in the project. They are perhaps the stakeholder groups most readily recognized. For publicly funded projects the number of stakeholders who can be identified is high. These generally consist of the following:

- Funders, whether this be a government department, grant provider or private sector partner.
- Users, whether these be passengers for a transport project or visitors for a museum.
- Regulatory authorities, most commonly the planning authorities, but also specialist regulatory authorities, for example those involved in rail projects.
- Those affected, who may be neighbours or those working or living nearby.
- The press and media are another significant group who can greatly influence perception of the project and its perceived, and in some cases actual, success.

It is relatively easy to identify 40 individual stakeholder groups for a significant public project, although private sector projects tend to have slightly fewer. One of the key problems with stakeholder management is the sheer number of people involved and the fact that their levels of power and interest differ markedly. Management of the stakeholder environment is a highly complex management task.

7.2.3 Stakeholder analysis

Stakeholder analysis can be used to understand the stakeholder environment and priorities to management resources. It can be undertaken as follows: the first step is to identify stakeholders, you cannot manage them if you do not know who they are, list them out. This exercise will need to involve all members of the team. Next decide on the level of power and interest each individual stakeholder has to influence the project. This is not a precise art, the assessment can only be based on the perceptions of the team, but it is important that you consider "interest" from their point of view not yours, a large organization, for example a key grant provider, may be of great interest to the project but is the project of great interest to the grant provider? If the project does not happen they can just fund something else. You then plot the stakeholders on a matrix. You will then need to define whether the individual stakeholder groups are broadly positive or negative about the project. You will probably find that those with a high level of interest, on the right of the matrix are either strongly supportive or otherwise; this is not surprising as their interest is high and so they have an opinion. Those on the left may have no strongly formed views.

This completes the basic analysis; you should then use the analysis to form the basic management and communication strategy for the project.

7.2.4 Active management of stakeholders

The basic requirement is to manage the project so that positive stakeholders are in the bottom right-hand corner and negative stakeholders are out of that corner. You need to remember that the matrix is dynamic, changes of individual within stakeholder organizations or changes to your project will be reflected in the matrix. The following are some ideas for strategies that you or the client may wish to adopt to deal with the various groups.

7.2.4.1 High power, high interest

If they are positive provide them with information to maintain their support, look after them well they are important, let them know that. Do not ignore them just because they are not causing you any problems at the moment. Involve them in your project, make them part of your project steering group (if they are not already), involve them in decisions, use them to lobby other groups and make sure they voice their support. Those with high power and interest, who are negative, are a big problem and you need to put effort into dealing with them. Use other positive stakeholders to lobby them and hopefully change their views, attempt to counter any negative influence they may have on other groups, reduce their power if the means exists to do this. They may also respond to bargaining. Find out what is important to them, help them out, buy their favour. Some also respond to information and interest.

Management strategies
Positive

- Provide information to maintain their support
- Consult with them prior to taking project decisions
- Meet with them regularly
- Consult with them, involve them, and seek to build their confidence in the project and the team
- Encourage them to act as advocates for the project
- Nurture them, look after them, they are critically important to you and to the project.

Negative

- Attempt to develop their support and change their view by ensuring they fully understand the project and the benefits it will deliver. Their resistance may be due to lack of information or understanding.
- Attempt to build their confidence in you and in the team.
- Find out what is important to them, if you can help them out or minimize negative impact on them they may be more helpful.
- Demonstrate that you are doing your best to limit adverse effects on them.
- Counter any negative influence they may have on others.

7.2.4.2 High power, low interest

The high power, low interest group is the unexploded bomb and its interest is low, at the moment. However if the project alters or the individuals change their interest may suddenly increase and they will use their power to influence the project.

Management strategies
Positive

- Maintain their enthusiasm and interest in the project, they are good allies to have.
- Provide them with information, invite them to presentations, involve them as much as resources allow. This can be done fairly cheaply through a project website, newsletter, or open presentations.
- Seek their input and opinion if you can, this will flatter them, but ensure that you do not get too many opinions.

Negative

- This is a group that you will probably know all too well, because of their high level of interest they will probably deluge you (or your client) with e-mails and other correspondence. You need to be sure that you do not spend too much time on them, remember their power is low.
- You may need to get the project sponsor or client representative to take a firm line with them and they can use a lot of time and resource.

7.2.4.3 Low power, low interest

Make sure you do not spend too much time on them but if they are supportive provide them with information and be nice to them; their position or view may change in the future.

Management strategies

- Ensure they receive the project newsletter, have access to a project web site or are invited to presentations.

7.2.5 Conclusions

Like all management models, the key benefit of stakeholder analysis is that it helps bring understanding to a complex situation and therefore helps project managers and teams to manage and communicate with stakeholders in the most effective way, enabling them to concentrate resources where maximum benefit will be derived and informing communications planning for the project. The benefits are very much in the discipline of having undertaken the process. However stakeholder analysis is only a tool that helps the project manager and the team identify the management actions necessary. It is perhaps most easily applicable to the management of external stakeholders and a useful output of stakeholder analysis is a project communications plan which will help the team define and understand which stakeholders they need to communicate with and how. A typical format for a project communications plan is given below; the output of the stakeholder analysis exercise can be used to help define the recommended approach and action plan. On a large project this helps define clarity of communication routes and ensure consistency.

Management of internal stakeholders is if anything more complex because internal stakeholders are generally closer to the issues and will be affected to a greater degree. If we are to avoid large-scale change to project as it progresses it is important that we ensure that it is set up right in the first place with the right types of involvement and consultation. The important thing is to get the wider internal stakeholder group involved as early as possible. Involve them in the detail of the briefing process, present the initial designs to them, and take their comments seriously. Everyone must get a chance to learn about the project, have their say, hear about what others think, learn about the complexities and limitations of the project, and the opportunities it presents. Not everyone will get exactly what he/she wants, but they are more likely to accept what they do get if they know why a particular decision was made and if they feel they played a part in making that decision. This is a time-consuming process but it is important because it will smooth the path for the later stages of the project and it is the best way to ensure that the project optimizes benefit for the client organization. For example there may be the opportunity to streamline the project by sharing facilities rather than by satisfying individual wish lists and broader consultation will lead to better project briefing. These processes allow you to tap into the knowledge, skills, and creativity of a wider range of individuals.

The process obviously needs control, but communication should occur as freely as possible, and decisions made should be communicated to the wider group as efficiently as possible.

Free communication between designers and users, certainly in the early stages, allows the designers to build a better understanding of what they are designing for and allows users the opportunity to learn about what is achievable and what is not. The sort of communication route described in Figure 1 may well simplify the project management task and maximize the chances of delivering the project to cost and time but it is unlikely to assist in the delivery of the best project to meet the needs of the organization as well as possible.

Where a range of departments within an organization is affected by a particular project we need to give careful thought to how communication is managed. The project team is set up as a temporary team, who will probably move on after the project is finished, other departments in the organization know that they will have to live with the results. We need to ensure that the project is suitably integrated with the overall development of the organization. A project team that works in isolation may well deliver a project on budget and time as there has been little client led change but it is unlikely that they will deliver the project that the organization actually requires. It is important that information about the project, that will affect the whole organization, is cascaded out. One mechanism is to nominate project representatives in each of the departments affected who maintain communication.

It is important to remember that when we build, we are building not just for a single individual but also for a wide group of people who will have to live with the building when the project team has moved on. Rather than complaining that we cannot get clear decisions out of the client, we need to try to understand the range of needs to be satisfied and achieve an optimal balance. Project managers will probably always be judged on whether or not they delivered the project to time and budget and the more they need to involve project stakeholders in the process the greater the risk to time and budget; but if we are to deliver projects that meet the long-term needs of organizations we need to involve and meet the needs of the organizations' stakeholders and we can only do this through active stakeholder management.

(This essay is credited to Deborah Vogwell of Davis Langdon Everest and was presented at PMI Europe Congress 2003, and is reproduced with permission, Copyright Davis Langdon and Everest, 2004.)

7.3 Essay No. 3: Trends in Stakeholder Management and Measurement in the Public Sector

This research paper identifies how stakeholder management and measurement are changing in the public sector. It assesses how eight government departments are currently managing and measuring their stakeholders. It presents aspects of stakeholder management and measurement in each of the organizations through the eyes of the chief executive or another senior manager. The project identifies what is driving senior managers' actions and what is working most effectively, in order to inform others and spread good practice. The results show that some public sector managers are taking greater control of their stakeholder management by:

- appointing relationship managers
- formalizing their relationships with other departments
- establishing protocols and consulting representatives from community groups and population agencies
- actively marketing their initiatives, to raise awareness among the public and attract a response from interested parties
- recognizing the need for flexibility, as stakeholders change and new issues arise.

The main difference among senior managers is in the breadth of their definition of stakeholders. Some define the term narrowly, to include only those with whom they have immediate contact. One or two exclude their own staff, regarding them as an inherent part of the organization. But many of the managers interviewed have a broader definition that embraces wider evaluation issues.

Senior managers acknowledge that it has become more complex for them to measure their performance in this area and the effect of their actions. But many departments continue to rely upon internal and relatively informal performance assessment. Evaluation of some major interdepartmental initiatives is also at an early stage. As initiatives such as "strengthening families" are increasingly used as models for government action, there will be growing pressure not only to evaluate their success, but also to develop measures to benchmark and monitor stakeholder satisfaction.

7.3.1 The pressure for change

Many government departments have moved beyond the emphasis of the early 1990s on restructuring and cost reduction and are now concentrating on effectiveness. Their focus has shifted from outputs to outcomes, and to balancing economic and social elements in government policy. At the same time, the government's programme of change continues. Welfare reforms in the past 24 months have been greater than in the last 60 years.

Public sector managers are looking outwards, towards understanding the impact that their policies are making on New Zealand society. Government departments cannot conceive policy in a vacuum. Rather they must make a concerted effort to manage and measure their stakeholders' needs and expectations.

Government organizations have always had to understand and meet the needs of their various stakeholders: ministers, partners, clients, and customers. Stakeholder management is an iterative process that continues even while outcomes are being defined. But in the last 3 years interest in stakeholder management and measurement has grown.

Until recently the approach taken to stakeholder management by many government departments was relatively informal and unstructured. Information about stakeholders rested on impressions and anecdotes, rather than on measurement. However, many departments are now taking a more formal and systematic approach to managing their stakeholders, and in some cases, to measuring their stakeholders' perceptions.

Government organizations are under pressure to take greater control of their stakeholder relationships as a result of the following trends:

- *Consumerism*: Customers' and partners' service expectations have grown. Members of the public want greater control over their lives and the services they receive. As a result, government organizations have had to become more responsive to their customers and partners, and to the groups that represent them.
- *Proliferation of non-governmental organizations (NGOs)*: The number of voluntary organizations and other community groups is rapidly expanding, especially in response to changes in the government's role in health, education, and welfare.
- *Maori issues*: Government departments have to recognize and be responsive to issues arising from the Treaty of Waitangi.
- *Greater openness and communication*: The government has radically changed its approach to public consultation. Gone are the days when a Ministry, such as Foreign Affairs, never spoke to the press. Now the Ministry of Foreign Affairs and Trade has established networks with the press at division director level, and open communication with the public is the norm for all government departments. The Official Information Act puts considerable power into stakeholders' hands, giving them and their Members of Parliament (MPs) access to information that was previously unavailable.
- *The MMP environment*: The advent of minority government has led to growing numbers of portfolio ministers and

independent subcommittees. For instance, the Department of Labour now has four portfolio ministers, or eight if associate ministers are included. Since August 1997, the number of ministerial teams under MMP has trebled. As a coalition changes, new issues and stakeholders emerge.

- *Legislation*: It is a requirement to consult under legislation such as the Resource Management Act.
- *Government restructuring*: The reorganization of government departments has created new stakeholders and changed service delivery. For example, the creation of Work and Income NZ (WINZ) in October 1998 resulted in the integration of four bodies, each with previously distinct stakeholders: New Zealand Employment Service, Income Support, Community Employment Group and Local Employment Co-ordination. The new organization now offers service delivery through combined sites.
- *Increased co-operation with other agencies*: One of the most important trends in recent years has been the establishment of joint initiatives such as "strengthening families". "Strengthening families" involves co-operation between, among others, the Department of Social Welfare, the Ministries of Health and Education, local communities, and the police. These inter-departmental activities have tended to make stakeholder management and measurement more complex. But co-operation with other departments and the setting up of common frameworks has also led to shared gains and a clearer understanding of the contribution that other departments can make. Government departments are also increasingly co-operating by exchanging information and setting up common databases. This has led to the need for common standards and quality control.
- *Outsourcing*: Outsourcing of services is a growing trend in many government departments. For example, the Children Young Persons and Their Families Agency now contracts out all but its core services. A government department that outsourcers its services must have a clear understanding of its customers' future needs and manage its supplier relationships to ensure that its partners deliver consistent, high quality services to its customers.

7.3.2 Defining stakeholders

There is general recognition that stakeholder management involves balancing the needs of various constituencies. Each of these is seen to have a legitimate interest in the success or failure of a particular department, and each has the ability to help or hinder it in its mission.

The main difference among respondents is in the breadth of their definition of stakeholders. Some define stakeholders narrowly, to include only those with whom they have immediate contact. One or two exclude their own staff, regarding them as an inherent part of the organization. But many of the managers interviewed have a broader definition that embraces wider evaluation issues. Some extend the definition to include their department's impact on society as a whole; others believe that it is pretentious for government departments to seek societal impacts. The latter believe that it is the role of parliament to make such value judgements and that government officials are not accountable for the whole of society.

There is general agreement that two groups of stakeholders should receive priority attention: ministers and end-customers.

The range of stakeholders managed by a government organization is often diverse. For example, the Department of Labour's stakeholders include the following:

- *Ministers*: these can be either customers or owners
- *Customers*: these include both end-customers and others served by the department's field staff
- *Politicians*: these include MPs who represent both the customer and taxpayer interests of their constituents
- *Other government departments and crown entities*: these include the Treasury, the State Services Commission and Department of the Prime Minister and Cabinet
- *Other government departments*: these are organizations which share policy interests with the department, such as the Ministries of Commerce, Education, Research, Science and Technology, the Department of Social Welfare, Te Puni Kokiri, and the Ministries of Women's Affairs and Pacific Island Affairs
- *Agencies outside the state sector*: these include representatives of social groups such as the Employers' Federation, the Council of Trade Unions, the Manufacturers' Federation and Enterprise New Zealand, and single industry organizations, representing client groups on matters such as health and safety.

7.3.3 More proactive stakeholder management

Stakeholder management is absorbing a growing amount of the time and energy of chief executives. McCann research in 1998 indicates that of the 11 roles that CEOs fill, stakeholder management takes between 1% and 30% of their time. For some CEOs the time spent may be much greater. A "hands-on" chief executive, such as Margaret Bazley, Director General of the Ministry of Social Policy, may spend more than half her time talking to stakeholders such as mayors and other community leaders, corporate leaders, and the department's own staff. She generally allocates 1 day a week for visits out of the corporate office, and attends work-related meetings on most evenings. If the time spent with ministers, Treasury and the State Services Commission is included, up to 70% of her time is spent working with stakeholders, briefing them, listening, and keeping them on board.

Several other departments are taking more formal organization-wide action to control their stakeholder relationships. For example, in the past 5 years the Department of Labour has taken three main steps to strengthen its stakeholder management. These are:

- *Establishing a structure of relationship managers*: Each organization within the department has designated responsibility to a single manager for managing a stakeholder relationship and monitoring its health. This individual provides a point of contact, if a problem arises. The relationship managers report regularly on the quality of the relationships and share information with others in the management team, so that the department can take appropriate action when required.
- *Formalizing stakeholder relationships*: The department has monthly meetings at both chief executive and senior management level with other organizations such as the Department of Social Welfare and ACC. These meetings cover issues such as policy, service delivery, human resource management policies, and IT development. They also provide a useful fail-safe mechanism, ensuring that issues are not missed and that any personal differences at senior level do not result in a breakdown of communication.
- *Agreeing protocols*: The department has established formal protocols with organizations such as Te Puni Kokiri and the Ministry of Pacific Island Affairs, setting out the relationship between them.

Following its recent restructuring, WINZ has established an account management team to handle its stakeholder relationships. WINZ has three full-time "account managers" at national office. They have three main roles:

- Handling governance issues, such as memoranda of understanding and protocols with population agencies

- Managing day-to-day interdepartmental matters, to help ensure a "no surprises" environment
- Developing agreements, such as negotiating purchase agreements.

The account managers' goal is to resolve any interdepartmental disputes between officials, so that they do not escalate to senior management. All other WINZ sections also have their own points of contact. For example, both the policy and communication teams deal directly with their counterparts in other departments.

Stakeholder management at WINZ is complex. Managing relationships with the purchase and policy advisers (Departments of Labour and Social Welfare) is unusually complicated because WINZ is both a provider/purchase of services and an operational policy adviser. For example, potential conflict between its roles can arise when ministers seek assistance. Is the response they receive advice, information or a recommendation to act?

WINZ identifies three main types of stakeholders:

- Purchase and policy advisers (the Departments of Social Welfare and Labour)
- Central agencies (the Treasury, the State Services Commission, and the Department of Prime Minister and Cabinet)
- Population agencies (Te Puni Kokiri and the Ministries of Pacific Island Affairs, Youth Affairs, and Women's Affairs).

The account managers have regular weekly meetings and daily contact with the Departments of Social Welfare and Labour. They take part in fortnightly meetings with the central agencies, to which they invite senior managers from areas such as human resources, communications, case management, IT, and finance. Between meetings they co-ordinate the handling of enquiries. They are also establishing a more proactive approach to the population agencies, to obtain more information on the needs of WINZ's customers.

One of the most successful initiatives that the account managers have introduced is taking key stakeholders on 1- or 2-day visits to see WINZ in action, for instance at its new integrated customer service sites.

The account management approach has led other agencies to reorganize their own relationship management structures, to match the arrangement at WINZ. Although the new account management structure is generally working well, the department finds itself less well resourced than its partners, particularly as the account managers are often asked to assist with other matters, such as data sharing.

The agency identifies four main stakeholder groups:

- NGOs
- Maori and Pacific Island communities
- Providers from whom the agency contracts services
- Family home caregivers.

The agency has frequent contact with its reference groups, which provide advice on service provision and policymaking and are actively involved in its strategy development and business planning. The agency formally meets Maori and Pacific Island reference groups every 2 months and has regular meetings with the Family Services reference group, which includes representatives from Barnardo's and Open Home. The agency also has frequent informal contact with iwi, since it contracts services direct from 13 iwi around the country.

The treasury has a highly systematic approach to its relationships with other government departments, and clearly differentiates levels of responsibility. It appoints a middle manager to safeguard the relationship with each department. The treasury has established the nature and type of formal feedback that it requires throughout the year. However, it is also keen to develop an approach based on evaluating key events and activities, and piloting this approach with one department.

The treasury has also found that departments with which it has more frequent contact have a better understanding of its role and tend to be more positive about its policies. It is, therefore, planning to take a more proactive role, to broaden the level of involvement with its stakeholders.

7.3.4 Shifting the balance of power

The process of stakeholder management alters radically when a government department embarks on a major programme of social change. Initiatives, frequently involving joint action with other government departments, may set out deliberately to change stakeholder expectations and responsibilities.

Such a change in stakeholder management is evident at the Ministry of Education, which has the ambitious goal of shifting the balance of power from the centre to its stakeholders in schools and the community. This has not been universally accepted and old habits die-hard.

The CEO acts as the surrogate employer of teachers, but it is unclear who is responsible for the teacher relationship. Building on the devolution achieved under "Tomorrow's Schools", the ministry aims to implement a change programme which will integrate education more closely with social policy. To assess its effectiveness, the Ministry is looking more broadly at educational and social outcomes rather than relying upon the traditional, narrower measures of individual school performance.

The ministry is undertaking a series of trial initiatives in areas with schools that have traditionally performed poorly. These include projects in South Auckland, on the East Coast in partnership with Ngati Porou, and among the Tuhoe people.

The Ministry's goal is to bring schools and communities together. The onus is on schools to develop their own strategies, supported by both staff and parents, before they can receive funding. The Ministry also wants parents to take ownership of the initiatives and to help shape the school environment. This has had a profound impact on the relationship between the Ministry and its stakeholders. The change process strengthens the roles of teachers, principals, boards, and parents. It breaks dependency on the Ministry and therefore reduces central control.

The strategies can also lead to the creation of new stakeholder groups and different structures, such as the clustering of schools in a geographical area, common school boards, or the setting up of a new local educational authority.

The Ministry recognizes the importance of helping those in education to enhance their own relationship management skills, including managing change, setting values, listening, and intelligence gathering.

The ambitious programme has a number of implications for stakeholder management.

1. The Ministry recognizes the need to think through in advance the implications of policy implementation. Will those at the receiving end be able to manage policy? What assistance do they need in relationship management? How will the community react? What is the best way to explain the Ministry's goals and to communicate with stakeholders?

2. It is important to recognize variation and the need to provide diverse governance arrangements. The Ministry is moving away from a "one-size-fits-all" approach to an enabling environment for individual communities, which necessitates working closely with those on the ground and tailoring programmes to local needs.

3. It needs to balance empowerment with financial accountability. The Ministry's goal is to change its approach to school funding, from financial gap filling to putting school learning on a firm footing. It aims to spend money and use resources in a smarter way. Although the initiatives involve a transfer of power and resources, accountability to parliament is retained.

4. The approach has impacted on how schools report to stakeholders in their communities and the need for transparency of information. Communicating information on matters such as the children's progress, what a 9-year-old child can do, national benchmarks, and leading-edge practice has to be transparent.

5. The programme has to accommodate huge swings of emotion, as the attitude of the community typically moves from depression through an unleashing of enthusiasm to tensions when the project is evaluated. Changes in stakeholders' attitudes and motivation have to be anticipated and managed.

6. Finally, the Ministry has to balance self-determination with the need for intervention and devise effective exit strategies. It has to build up sufficient capability to monitor a school's performance so that it can respond quickly and provide the necessary support.

7.3.5 Potential pitfalls in managing stakeholders

Departments may encounter a number of potential pitfalls in managing their stakeholders. Those identified include the following issues:

7.3.5.1 Failing to identify stakeholders

Usually it is relatively simple to identify a department's stakeholders. But in some circumstances, especially when launching an initiative or campaign, some stakeholders are not obvious. Stakeholders can also change as the political agenda changes. Some individuals and organizations may remain dormant and then arise unexpectedly. (An example of unidentified stakeholders was the late intervention by Maori stakeholders in the recent GATT trade negotiations, claiming intellectual property rights.) Other individuals may claim influence, but may not represent the groups they claim to stand for.

The Ministry of Foreign Affairs and Trade reduces the risk of failing to identify stakeholders by undertaking a campaign to raise public awareness of their initiatives. This involves putting forward public documentation, marketing it, making public speeches about the issues, and seeking public views. Obtaining the minister's support for this approach in advance is essential. The Ministry then listens to stakeholders' responses. If individuals or groups do not identify themselves, they cannot expect to have a say.

7.3.5.2 Losing control

It is essential to understand the balance of power in any stakeholder relationships, and in particular not to confuse the process of seeking "consultation" with "agreement". Greater attention to stakeholders is not necessarily good, if stakeholders are allowed to capture the agenda. Stakeholders can paralyse negotiations if discussions move from consultation to acceding to stakeholders' demands. Government must retain final control, as it is ultimately accountable to the general public through the electoral process.

7.3.5.3 Failing to recognize that some stakeholders' views are irreconcilable

Some stakeholders are ideologically driven and it may not be possible to reconcile their views with a department's actions. It is necessary to listen to their views, and to ensure maximum damage limitation, but not to extend consultation to the power of veto.

7.3.5.4 Dealing with stakeholder jealousy

A perceived imbalance between stakeholder power and influence may lead to friction. Some stakeholders can become very concerned if they believe others are receiving greater attention from government.

7.3.5.5 Recognizing dual accountability

When public servants are appointed as stakeholder representatives, they sometimes find they have a conflict of interest between their duties to the public service and their perceived obligations to the communities they represent.

7.3.5.6 Handling ministerial mismanagement of stakeholders

Some ministers manage their own stakeholder responsibilities poorly. If the resulting criticism falls upon a government department, it is often difficult to handle and can cause considerable tension.

7.3.5.7 Working within the political environment

In the private sector, managers normally behave rationally according to their own interests. But in the public sector, the overlay of the political environment means that ministers are sometimes subject to pressures and influences that may result in a non-rational response. If the government lacks a coherent overall political strategy, it can become impossible for public servants to introduce consistent, effective measures at departmental level.

7.3.6 Stakeholder measurement

7.3.6.1 Stakeholder relationship measurement

The extent of stakeholder measurement varies from one government department to another. Some departments conduct regular end-customer satisfaction studies and some undertake surveys of the relationship with their ministers. For example, the Department of Labour conducts 6-monthly surveys of the perceptions of its ministers, and at least annual surveys of its field customers.

However, compared with the private sector, formal measurement of other stakeholder relationships is limited. For example, many companies routinely measure their relationships with their business partners and commission independent reviews of their account managers' performance. Some companies are actively reviewing whether their annual reports should include "stakeholder dialogue" and quantified assessments of performance with each interested stakeholder group, as well as the traditional profit and loss statement.

Some of the government departments interviewed are planning to introduce more formal stakeholder relationship measures. For example, the Children Young Persons and Their Families Agency does not currently conduct end-customer surveys, but plans to do so when it has firmer outcome measures. The account managers at WINZ currently have no formal performance measures in their new structure, but recognize that these could be useful.

Other organizations such as the New Zealand Police have undertaken a wide range of performance measures. The police have a strategy to move more resource and focus towards prevention of crime. Recognizing that it cannot do so alone, and that it is unlikely to secure resources for that purpose alone, it has engaged in several key processes:

- An extensive review that aims to shift more resource to the "front-line"
- Dialogue and robust debate with stakeholders in the road safety, emergency management, and criminal justice sectors
- Alignment of strategic direction with sector partners in order that efficiencies can be identified and resources aligned to key resource areas
- A quality policing programme that restores local partnerships so that police are part of communities and not apart from them.

The police have introduced extensive measures, including programme balancing processes and results.

7.3.7 Measuring outcomes

Evaluating the outcomes of initiatives, such as "strengthening families", is at an early stage. Policy staff at the Department of Social Welfare are currently working on how to measure and monitor the success of the programme, but indications are that it may become a model for future joint initiatives.

Evaluation of the Ministry of Education's regional initiatives is also as yet unsystematic. In South Auckland, a group from Auckland University is conducting an Action Research Project, and the Education Review Office is undertaking discretionary school audits. In time, the ministry plans to benchmark performance with national norms.

While it is relatively straightforward to define outcomes, it is harder to measure them. Outcomes are long term and often involve interdepartmental teams. Government departments do not have full control over events, and political actions can override the initiatives they take. Evaluating initiatives and their impact on stakeholders is therefore one of the major challenges facing government departments, especially if interdepartmental initiatives become the model for future government innovation.

7.3.8 Conclusion

In the last 3 years public sector interest in stakeholder management has grown, as the number of stakeholders for many government departments has increased and stakeholders' expectations have continued to rise. Greater consultation and more transparent communication are now essential. The traditional view that persuading the public was the responsibility of ministers rather than public officials has changed. Now it is also the job of government departments to communicate and explain their policies to the public.

Some public sector managers are responding to the pressures from stakeholders by taking greater control of their stakeholder management, appointing relationship managers, and formalizing their relationships with other departments. Increasingly, they are establishing protocols and formally consulting representatives from population agencies, such as Te Puni Kokiri and the Ministry of Women's Affairs and other government agencies and NGOs. They recognize the need for flexibility, as stakeholders change and new issues arise. Some departments are aware of the potential problem of failing to identify stakeholders, and are actively marketing their initiatives, to raise awareness among the public and attract a response from interested parties.

The main difference among senior managers is in the breadth of their definition of stakeholders. Some define stakeholders narrowly, to include only those with whom they have immediate contact. One or two exclude their own staff, regarding them as an inherent part of the organization. But many of the managers interviewed have a broader definition that embraces wider evaluation issues.

The extent of stakeholder measurement varies by government department. Some departments conduct regular end-customer satisfaction studies and undertake surveys of the relationship with their ministers. Some are considering introducing new customer surveys and performance measures. But many departments continue to rely upon internal performance assessment, and informal feedback from their stakeholders. Evaluation of some major initiatives is still at a relatively early stage.

Looking forward, the trend is towards more interdepartmental initiatives, and a greater use of partnering and outsourcing. For many government departments the challenge will be to prioritize and link these programmes, integrate them in a risk management plan and ensure that they are aligned with stakeholders' needs. This will require sophisticated and timely evaluation methodologies. It will also call for the introduction of investigative research and performance measures.

We believe stakeholder research has an important role to play in benchmarking and monitoring the satisfaction of a range of stakeholder groups. In particular, it can help government departments to:

- prioritize outcomes, by seeking stakeholders' perceptions of a department's activities and how these should be focused
- identify and understand the views of NGOs and other community groups, especially in response to initiatives in health, education, and welfare
- provide an independent assessment of the performance of partners and other organizations to which customer services are outsourced
- audit the relationship between a department and its main stakeholders, especially when the performance of individual managers is assessed on their ability to manage these relationships.

(This essay is credited to Douglas Wood of the Consultancy Group NAVIGATE, Wellington, New Zealand and is reproduced with permission, Copyright NAVIGATE, 2004.)

Figure 7.1 Summarizes all three essays.

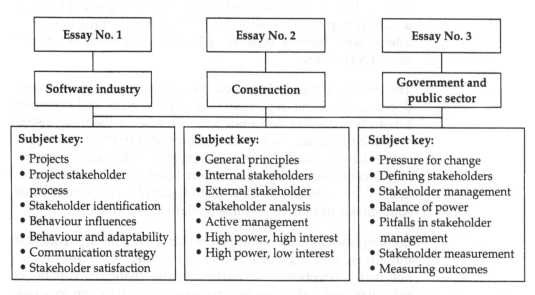

Figure 7.1 Stakeholder management, essay summary.

7.4 Biographies

7.4.1 Essay No. 1: Robin Dudash

Robin Dudash has 18 years experience in all levels of computing from business mainframes, client-server, to real-time process control platforms. Through her successful project management, she has led major capital expenditures budgeting in excess of $2 million. Some of these projects were fully automated control systems and contracted to attain 99.9% system reliability.

Ms. Dudash has been a Senior American Society for Quality (ASQ) Member since 1994 and the ASQ Pittsburgh Education Chair for the past 8 years. She has also taught a Certified Software Quality Engineering (CSQE) Refresher Course based on the ASQ Body of Knowledge. This course has realized a pass rate of 95% for the last 6 years, and is now available online. Ms. Dudash currently owns her own company that conducts consulting for ISO 9001 and sector-specific quality system development, training services, and internal quality auditing services. She is also a subcontracted Lead Assessor for a Registrar.

Prior assignments included Area Technical Manager for process control functions at for all strip finishing, which included 23 operating units, processing stainless and electrical coils from hot band to ship. Managing a team of engineers and welding and metallurgical technicians, efforts focused on identification and management of key process variables, continuous improvement projects, and resolution of customer complaints. While attending college and after college, she was a Systems Engineer developing optimized computer models for BOF charging and cold mill rolling performance at various steel operations for US Steel.

7.4.2 Essay No. 2: Deborah Vogwell

Deborah Vogwell is an architect and has worked as architect and project manager on a range of construction projects, including the role of Assistant Project Manager for the British Museum's £100 million Great Court project. She has an MBA from Cranfield University and currently works for construction consultancy Davis Langdon Everest, primarily developing and delivering services such as risk and value management. Many of the projects on which she is involved are large and involve numerous stakeholders, she has spent the last few years developing and implementing processes for managing stakeholders on projects. She also writes and lectures on risk and stakeholder management.

7.4.3 Essay No. 3: Douglas Wood

Douglas specializes in consulting and research in relationship management. He has conducted a range of projects identifying best practice and helping public sector bodies to manage their stakeholders effectively. Douglas has conducted workshops on stakeholder management planning, external and internal relationship management, and influencing skills training. He has undertaken stakeholder management projects for a wide range of government organizations, including central agencies, government departments. This work has included in-depth research interviews at Cabinet and chief executive levels. Douglas is also the author of a research paper, *Trends in Stakeholder Management and Measurement in the Public Sector in New Zealand.* Before setting up research write, Douglas was a Research Director at the Wellington offices of AC Nielsen.

Adoption   Taking up and practicing or using as one's own.

Appraisal   An estimation or analysis of a proposed project to determine its acceptability and merit according to established criteria.

Agreement   An arrangement or contract as to a course of action; the language or instrument embodying such a contract.

Assessment   Determination of the importance, size, or other characteristics of a projects needs, market opportunities.

Barriers   Factors that prevent or impede the project or practices.

Capacity building   Increasing skilled personnel and technical and institutional capacity.

Community-driven projects   Project transfers initiated and lead by community organizations and entities with a high degree of collective decision-making.

Co-operation   Association of persons or institutions for common benefit. Generally used to denote the collaboration for purposes of spreading practices or know-how.

Diffusion   The spread of practices or know-how from one area or group of people to others by contact.

Direct investment   Capital invested for the purpose of acquiring a long-term interest in an enterprise and of exerting a degree of influence on that enterprises' operations.

Evaluation   Periodic assessment of efficiency, performance, relevance, and impact of a project in the context of stated objectives. It is an objective examination assessing the meeting of tasks by the supplier, identifying best practice for further projects, resources required for the future and the need for future projects.

Full-cost pricing   The pricing of commercial goods that would include in the final prices faced by the end user not only the private costs of inputs, but also the costs of the externalities created by their production and use.

Government-driven projects   Projects initiated by governments who play a leading role in the transfer as well.

Implementation   Carrying out; giving practical effect to and ensuring of actual fulfilment of project transfer processes by concrete measures.

Innovation   The introduction of something new; a new idea, method, or device.

Intellectual property right   An intangible asset, such as a copyright or patent.

Invention   A device, contrivance, or process originated after study and experiment.

Joint implementation   Possible agreements between stakeholders and third party to provide and deliver goods and services.

Joint venture   An alliance between two or more entities to carry out a single business enterprise by pooling property, money, equipment, and/or know-how.

Market barriers   Conditions, which prevent or impede the transfer of cost-effective technologies or practices that could adapt to or mitigate climate change.

Market potential   The portion of the economic potential for adapting to or mitigation change that could be achieved under existing market conditions, assuming no new policies and measures.

Market-based incentives   Measures intended to directly change relative prices and overcome market barriers.

Mediation   A process in which a mediator assists and facilitates two or more parties to a controversy in reaching a mutually acceptable resolution of the controversy.

Mitigation   An intervention to reduce the risk associated with projects.

Milestones   Provide object verifiable indicators for short-term objectives facilitating measurement of achievements throughout a project rather than just at the end, indicating times when decisions will be made.

Monitoring A continuous assessment of project implementation in connection to the established timetables and the use of services, infrastructure, and inputs by project beneficiaries.

Monitoring report Report produced by the external monitor for the task manager, summarizing progress vs. the work plan of the project and underlining key issues for action by the task manager or other non-project bodies.

Project measures Measures whose benefits – such as improved performance but excluding the benefits of change mitigation – equal or exceed their costs. They are sometimes known as "measures worth doing anyway".

Objectives A description of the aim(s) of a project referring to activities, results, purpose, overall objectives, and goals.

Partnership Close co-operation between parties having specified and joint rights and responsibilities.

Project life cycle The process comprising different types of activities taking place at different times during the execution of the project.

Projects pathway A route through which technology transfer takes place, composed of a combination of processes and involving different stakeholders.

Policies Procedures developed and implemented by organizations regarding the goal of adapting to or mitigating change through the use of technologies and measures.

Regulatory measures Rules or codes enacted by governments that mandate product specifications or process performance characteristics.

Repetition A combination of efforts leading to transfer of a technology, including replication of a transfer project, reinvestment, and repurchase.

Replication The act or process of reproducing.

Stakeholder An individual who is materially affected by the outcome of the system. End users are often thought of as the primary stakeholders, but other stakeholders, such as shareholders and executive management, among others, also have a stake in the project.

Standards/performance criteria Set of rules or codes mandating or defining product performance (grades, dimensions, characteristics, test methods, and rules for use).

Technical potential The amount by which it is possible to address climate change by using a technology or practice in all applications in which it could technically be adopted, without consideration of its costs or practical feasibility.

Technology A piece of equipment, technique, practical knowledge or skills for performing a particular activity.

Technology transfer The broad set of processes covering the exchange of knowledge, money, and goods among different stakeholders that lead to the spreading of technology for adapting to or mitigating change in an attempt to use the broadest and most inclusive concept possible.

Terms of reference Definition of the requirements and objectives of the services requested under the terms of a contract or tender, including, where necessary, the methods and means to be used and/or results to be achieved.

Vulnerability The degree to which a systems is susceptible to, and unable to cope with, injury damage or harm.

Index